D1048791

SHOO A HA...

drawings by Jenny Plunkett   photography by Hugh Andrew

DAVE ARNOLD

A Manual
on how to Shoot a Handgun

Foreword by Dave Westerhout

DGUN

LIBRARY OF CONGRESS CATALOG CARD NUMBER: 83-90065

First published in 1979 by Ernest Stanton (Publishers) (Pty) Ltd, Nicholson Street, Denver, Johannesburg, South Africa.

First published in the United States of America in 1983.
Second Edition 1984.
Published in the United States of America and Canada by Dave Arnold by arrangement with Ernest Stanton (Publishers) (Pvt) Ltd and distributed by PVA Books, P.O. Box 2216, Canyon Country, California 91351.

This book may not be sold outside of the United States of America and Canada.

Cover Design: Ted Hoefsloot
Printed by: KNI incorporated, Anaheim, California
Typography: Impressions by Jaki, Anaheim, California

ISBN NUMBER:

ISBN Soft cover 0-9611108-1-3

ISBN Hard cover 0-9611108-2-1

Acknowledgements

I am indebted to the many people who have helped in the preparation of this book. Special thanks are due to Jenny Plunkett, the artist who drew the excellent illustrations, John Rae, who supplied the action photographs on which the drawings are based and Hugh Andrews, who has done all the photographic work that appears in this book. Bill Ford, Theo Martins and staff of MAN magazine and my publisher have given encouragement and valuable advice on lay out and presentation. Tony Whightman, Gavin Carson, Anthony White, Joe Hale and my wife Pat read the manuscript and gave constructive criticism that helped in the compiling of the final text.

My association with many shooting friends has added to my knowledge of pistol craft. They are so numerous that I hesitate to name individuals for fear of over looking others but Dave Westerhout, Alex MacFarlane, Tom Young, Eric Evans, Trevor Hull, Tony Weeks, Gavin Carson, Alex du Plessis, Lionel Smith, Tony Cross, Gerry Gore, Ray Chapman and Derek McClean deserve special mention. I also wish to thank Jerry Usher who, in a short space of time, changed my dogmatic views on shooting to a more flexible approach. My comrades of all ranks in the British South Africa Police, especially Peter Huson, Don Hollingworth and the late Dave Perkins, have also contributed to my knowledge of shooting as well as developing my responsibility with firearms. I owe a great deal to Clive Bloom who offered me encouragement and advice in my earlier attempts at writing.

All that is known about pistol shooting techniques has been pioneered by men like Ed McGivern, Elmer Keith, Bill Jordan, Maj-Gen Julian Hatcher, Jeff Cooper, Paul B Wesson and others who are listed in the Bibliography. I have no hesitation in stating that most of the shooting methods described have been devised by these men.

Probably every author owes much to his immediate family and I am no exception. My wife and two daughters have given me all the encouragement possible as well as making many sacrifices during the period that this book was written. Finally, my greatest debt of gratitude is to the late Captain S.F. Treharne of Port Elizabeth, to whom this book is dedicated. At the age of 80 this grand old man of shooting coached Grey College cadets in rifle markmanship and spent many hours teaching me most of what I know about firearms and how to use them. Without this knowledge, this book could never have been written.

Contents

Foreword

I first had the pleasure of meeting David Arnold twenty years ago through a shared interest in shooting.

I have always valued David's opinion on shooting matters and, in particular, I have always been conscious of the fact that he is one of the few skilled shooting authorities who has been prepared to spend a great deal of time and effort in the administration of shooting. To this day he remains forever prepared to help and coach novice and expert alike and his unselfish approach has probably prevented his being able to develop his own true potential as a competitor.

There are many excellent specialized books on target and practical pistol shooting which cater reasonably well for the enthusiast and expert. Such books are of necessity too advanced and specialized for the novice and may indeed be confusing. Anyone who has listened to Practical Pistol shooters discussing the merits of two well known makes of pistol will readily understand the problem. To cover all the specialized knowledge and take cognisance of all the differing opinions would require a work rivalling the *Encyclopaedia Britannica*.

What has been needed for a long time is a simplified book which introduces the reader to pistol ownership and through careful explanation of the basic principles can assist him or her to become a safe and competent handler of a pistol. This book caters for this need admirably and has then led the reader further into the more specialized knowledge required for competitive pistol shooting. Most top pistol shooters will tell you that their interest and skills developed in the same order that follows in the format of this book.

This book should help many novices to enjoy pistol shooting through different levels of skill and there will be few experts who will not learn something by pursuing its easily read chapters.

DAVID WESTERHOUT
Salisbury — May 1979
1977 World Practical Pistol Champion

Chapter One

HOW TO USE THIS BOOK

The purpose of this book is to help the reader learn how to use his, or her, pistol safely, effectively and within the law. This will not be achieved by reading through this work once and then returning it to the bookshelf to gather dust. The book should first be read through to get an overview of the subject even though there may be certain aspects that may not concern the reader. Each chapter that is applicable to the reader's needs should then be studied and what has been learnt put into practice on the range.

The sequence of instruction follows that used by the author in teaching police and civilians how to shoot a handgun. It is important to follow the same order as the more advanced techniques should only be attempted after the basics of pistol shooting have been thoroughly mastered. Obviously, those aspects that the reader will not use can be skipped.

None of the methods of shooting described in the pages that follow are new. All are accepted techniques of shooting and, where there is more than one method, all have been described with their pros and cons. Here the reader must experiment and decide which method suits his, or her, needs best. All too often writers on pistol shooting tend to be dogmatic in their views on what are the best handguns and shooting techniques. In most cases what they recommend may be best for them but not necessarily everyone.

While on the subject of shooting techniques, those who are only interested in learning how to defend themselves with a pistol should select the simplest technique possible. For those who intend to put in the necessary practice, the more advanced methods may well appeal and, while they may take a little longer to master, the time taken to learn them is invariably well worth it.

Hopefully, the reader will be able to obtain instruction from either a shooting club or a professional instructor. In most instances, at least one of the shooting styles described will be taught by the instructor and the book can be used to supplement such instruction.

Although the sporting side of pistol shooting is covered, most of the book has been devoted to the defensive aspects as the majority of readers will probably be interested in learning how to protect themselves. It is indeed unfortunate that, in spite of all the technological advances, the world seems to be becoming a more dangerous place to live in. International terrorism knows no bounds and violent crime is on the increase. The result is that many citizens have a need to possess a handgun as a means of protection but, regrettably, very few gun owners have any idea of how to use their pistols safely, let alone effectively. Of the few that do, most are enthusiasts.

Unless one is prepared to learn how to use a handgun, one is better off without one.

This book is really aimed at average handgun owners and, if it assists them in becoming proficient in the use of their pistols, the time spent in compiling this work will have been more than justified.

Chapter Two

HANDGUNS AND HOW THEY WORK

ome of the terminology used to describe the various types of handguns
d their component parts will be new to most beginners, and unless un-
rstood, much of what is written in this book will be completely mean-
gless. Having at least a basic knowledge of pistols and how they work is
cessary before learning how to handle and shoot them. Perhaps the
siest way of doing this is to look, very briefly, at the history of firearm
velopment.

It is not certain who first invented firearms and used them as weapons in
ttle. Gunpowder was known in Europe before 1267, being mentioned in
e writings of the monk Roger Bacon, although there is some evidence
at it may have been in existence as early as 846. It is also possible that
npowder was known to the ancient Chinese, and used by them as a
eapon of war, probably in the form of a rocket guided to the target by
ing fired from a bamboo tube.

The first firearms were very simple, being no more than a tube, closed at
e end. Gunpowder was poured into the open end and a ball or some
milar missile was rammed down tightly on top of the mixture. Gunpow-
r has the characteristic of burning extremely rapidly and, when a glowing
nber or coal was inserted down a small hole at the rear of the tube, the
essure from the burning gases was soon great enough to drive the missile
wn the barrel with considerable force. The early guns were made in a
imber of sizes, some being large siege guns or cannon used to demolish
tifications while others were much smaller and could be fired while
ing held in the hand. The manufacture of these weapons was extremely
de and often they were more dangerous to the user than to the enemy.

To be of any real value as a weapon some means of making firearms
ailable for immediate use had to be found. It is probably true to say that
e subsequent development of firearms is as much due to finding better
thods of igniting the powder as anything else. The great improvements

in the design of guns has invariably occurred only after a better system of ignition had been discovered.

The first attempt at devising a firing mechanism was the 'matchlock' which consisted of nothing more than a device for holding a glowing taper that was forced into the hole at the rear of the tube — now called the barrel — by means of a lever type of trigger. While it was a better method of firing a firearm, it had the disadvantage of always having to ensure that the taper or wick was burning.

The 'wheel-lock' was the first method of creating artificial fire in the form of sparks and was probably first used in Germany about 1515. The mechanism consisted of a wheel which was wound up against a spring somewhat similar to that of a clock. When the trigger was pulled, it caused the spring tension to rotate the wheel against a flint and the sparks that resulted ignited powder in a pan over the hole in the rear of the barrel, firing the weapon. The method of using a flint was further improved with the invention of the 'flintlock'. Here the flint was held in a device called a 'cock' (because it resembled a cockerel's head) or hammer. To fire, the hammer was pulled back, or cocked, against a strong spring and held in place by the trigger. Pulling the trigger released the hammer causing it to fall, striking the flint against a piece of metal known as a 'frizzen' which caused sparks to fire the weapon in the same way as the 'wheel-lock'.

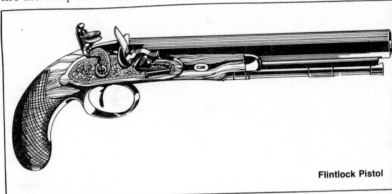

Flintlock Pistol

The inventions of the wheel-lock and flintlock permitted the general design of firearms to be improved. The weapons became lighter, better made and stocks to fit against the shoulder made them easier to fire and shoot. Guns that could be held in the hand came into existence during the 15th and 16th centuries and were called pistols. It is thought that the word originates from the Italian town of Pistoia, where many hand-held weapons were made from the year 1540 onwards, although it might also come from a French word meaning pipe. Today the word pistol is used to describe any firearm that can be fired with one hand. The word handgun is also used to describe such weapons.

The accuracy of pistols and shoulder weapons was much improved when, during 1500, German gunsmiths began to cut spiral grooves inside the barrels of their guns which became known as 'rifles'. Before, the inside gun barrels, called bores, had been smooth and rifling greatly improved both the accuracy and range of firearms by causing the missile or bullet to spin when it left the barrel.

Ironically, one of the greatest advances in ignition systems was due entirely to the efforts of a Scottish clergyman, Alexander John Forsyth who, in 1807, registered a patent for his percussion cap. The invention consisted of a small metallic cup containing fulminate of mercury, a chemical compound which explodes on impact. Forsyth used a similar type of lock to the Flintlock except that the percussion cap was placed over a small protrusion in place of the pan near the rear of the barrel. When struck by the hammer the fulminate of mercury exploded, driving a flash of flame down the hole in the centre of the nipple to fire the powder inside the barrel. The percussion cap not only made firearms more reliable but was quicker to load and fire and paved the way for repeating firearms.

For centuries the design of a reliable repeating firearm had been attempted without success. The first multi-shot firearms simply had additional barrels and firing mechanisms fitted but they were both heavy and cumbersome. An early repeating handgun was the 'pepperbox', a pistol with a single firing mechanism that served a number of rotating barrels. Once again the size and weight of the design killed it. The principle of having a revolving chamber had been known for some time prior to 1800

Percussion Pistol

but it took Forsyth's percussion cap and the ingenuity of a young American inventor, Samuel Colt to produce the first reliable revolver. In 1836 Colt patented his revolver design and, although difficulty in marketing them was initially experienced, he improved on his design and was soon producing them for sale throughout America and the Western World.

Colt's name has since become synonymous with revolvers which have changed little over the years other than minor improvements to the original design. Colt made use of a large drum or cylinder which held five or six separate chambers containing percussion cap, powder and bullets. The cylinder was placed between the hammer and the rear of the barrel and, by cocking back the hammer, the cylinder rotated enough to bring a loaded chamber in line with the barrel. The pistol was fired by pulling the trigger and then had to be re-cocked to repeat the process. This method of having to cock back the hammer for each shot is known as 'single action shooting' and revolvers that use this type of mechanism are called 'single actions'.

When Colt's patent expired others turned to manufacturing revolvers but he was still able to remain ahead in the field of firearm manufacture. This was due mainly to Colt revolvers being well made, accurate and reliable even though they were mass-produced. Although his name will always be linked with the revolver he was ahead of his time in many other ways. He foresaw the value of mass-production as well as the need to have

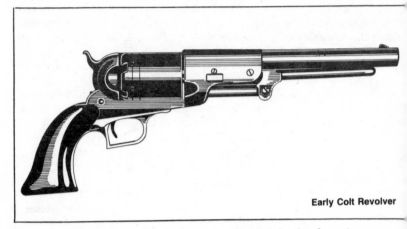

Early Colt Revolver

contented labour force. For the latter, he ensured that his factories were well planned and comfortable to work in as well as providing his employees with many other benefits. During the American Civil War his company turned out vast quantities of revolvers and other arms for the Union Forces. He died in 1862, aged 48, while devoting all his energies to the cause of the Union. His revolvers were popular, not only with the soldiers of the Union army, but also the Confederates who considered any Colt revolver snatched on the battlefield a prize worth its weight in gold.

One of the main improvements to Colt's single action revolvers was the double action. This mechanism, which permitted a revolver to be fired by just pulling the trigger, was introduced to England in 1851 by Robert Adams. He produced very strong, solid-framed revolvers which he further improved by buying patent rights of Frederick Beaumont that allowed them to be fired single action as well. Double action revolvers, which are sometimes called self-cockers, raise the hammer and turn the cylinder by pulling back the trigger. This allows them to be carried safely and ready for instant action. Although they are a much better design than the single action, it was only after the turn of the century that their true value as defence weapons was realised. Most modern revolvers can be fired either double or single action.

In the 1850s two American gunsmiths, Horace Smith and Daniel Wesson perfected a self-contained cartridge. In 1856 they bought the right to manufacture revolvers with the cylinder chambers bored right through. Ironically they obtained this patent from a Colt employee, Rollin White, nd when Colt's patent rights expired in 1857 they were in a position to manufacture cartridge firearms until 1869. Their first cartridge was a .22 short rimfire, little different from that of today. They were later able to make larger center fire cartridges and both of their designs are basically the same as modern cartridge ammunition.

The rimfire cartridge, which today is very popular in .22 caliber, consists of a copper or brass cartridge case, open at the front, which has its priming compound spun into the rim of its base. The case contains the

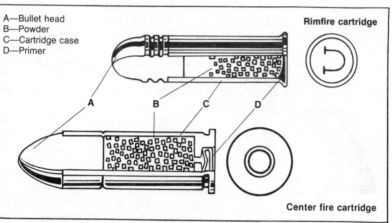

A—Bullet head
B—Powder
C—Cartridge case
D—Primer

Rimfire cartridge

Center fire cartridge

owder and the open end is plugged by the bullet. The center fire cartridge basically the same except that it has a percussion cap, called a primer, tted into the center of its base. Both are fired when either the rim or the rimer is struck by a pin, known as the 'firing pin' that is fitted to the front f the hammer.

Modern ammunition has a lot of terminology. As already mentioned, the percussion cap of a center fire cartridge is called a primer. The cartridge se is often referred to simply as case although some call it brass. The bullet ead is usually called a bullet or abbreviated to heads. A bullet can also refer a complete cartridge although the more common term used is 'a round'.

Caliber determines the diameter either of a bullet or the bore of the gun at fires it. In handguns, calibers range from the smallest of .22 to .476 and n be measured in hundreths of an inch, e.g. .22 or in millimetres, e.g. mm. Although rimfire refers to ammunition with the priming compound spun into its base, rounds may also be rimmed or rimless. The rmer refers to ammunition that has its base protruding above the diameter of the case and is used in revolvers. Rimless ammunition has its base arallel with the case with just a groove cut into the rear and is used in mi-automatic firearms.

If a pistol is being bought for self protection, some idea of the potency f its ammunition should be obtained. As regards accuracy, a modern well ade handgun will deliver far greater accuracy than most people can shoot. is quite possible to hit a man-size target at 100 yards and some of the ore powerful pistols can be shot at greater ranges. The old Colt percussion revolvers were surprisingly accurate up to great distances.

Even though handguns are accurate, since most attacks occur at very close range, often at night, there is rarely time to fire a well-aimed shot. For this reason a handgun bullet must have sufficient power to bring an attacker down even if a fatal wound has not been inflicted. The ability of a bullet to do this is called 'stopping power'.

Stopping power or knock-down power, as it sometimes is called, depends upon the velocity (speed) that a bullet travels, its shape, weight and caliber. The physical and mental state of the attacker is also relevant. A soldier would be difficult to stop during the heat and excitement of battle, while a person who is shot unexpectedly, may drop to the ground from shock even though the wound may not be fatal. The placement of the shot is also important. An attacker who is hit in a vital area that proves immediately fatal will be effectively stopped, regardless of the size of the bullet. Usually a hit in the trunk area of an assailant will put him down, even if not fatal, provided a bullet of reasonable caliber is used.

There is much argument as to which calibers are best for defense and, as there are so many factors to consider, it is difficult to come to any definite conclusion. The most extensive examination into this aspect of ballistics (science of moving projectiles) was carried out by the United States Army in the early part of this century to try to establish which was the best bullet for military pistols. Tests with every type of pistol ammunition then available indicated that the weight and caliber of bullets were more important than velocity. It was established that the best bullets for defense were those of the caliber of .41 and above.

Since then there have been considerable advances in ammunition design and manufacture. There are now various bullet designs and shapes that provide alternatively, good penetration or knockdown power, depending upon what is required. The magnum calibers are very powerful rounds that provide both penetration and great stopping power. As a general rule, the miniumum calibers suitable for defense are .38 Special for revolvers and 9 mm for semi-automatic pistols. Anything less will not guarantee stopping an assailant.

After the introduction of the self–contained metallic cartridge Smith and Wesson formed a company that produced many fine revolvers. These were of the break–top or tip–up type, having a frame that hinged in the middle which, when broken, ejected all empty cases simultaneously and was very quick to load. This type of design is still fairly common in revolvers, particularily those made by the British firm of Webley and Scott.

After Smith & Wesson's patent to manufacture cartridge revolvers expired, Colt produced their famous Model P Single Action Army revolver. This was adopted by the American Army in the early 1870s and became the most popular revolver in the Wild West. It was the favourite choice of all the famous Frontier characters and its popularity continued well into the 20th century. Its success was due to its simplicity, balance and ease of handling. Colt continued to make the Single Action Army, also called the 'Peacemaker' or 'Frontier Six Shooter' up until the beginning of the Second World War. After the war the demand for this revolver was s

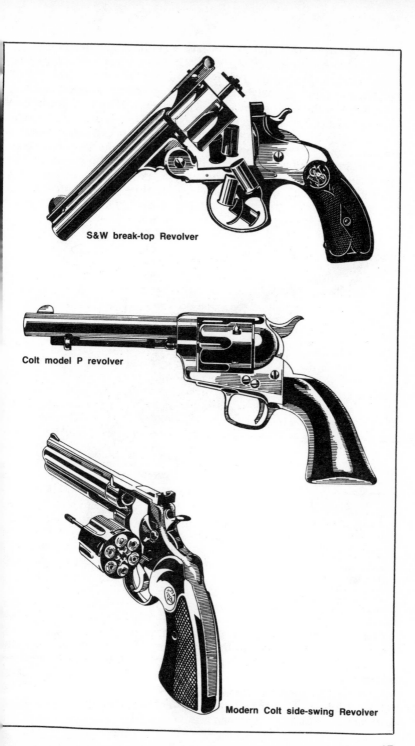

S&W break-top Revolver

Colt model P revolver

Modern Colt side-swing Revolver

great that Colt were forced to start manufacturing it again and it continued to be in production until 1982.

Towards the end of the 19th century double action revolvers became popular and both Colt and Smith & Wesson produced several designs that culminated in the solid frame side swing types that are still produced in various forms today. These revolvers have the strength of a solid frame yet can be quickly loaded and unloaded due to the cylinder swinging out to the side on a crane. An ejector-rod is provided to help remove the empty cases.

Most modern revolvers follow this design and, although the revolver is an old design, it is still a very good defense weapon because of its reliability, simplicity and speed in which it can be brought into action.

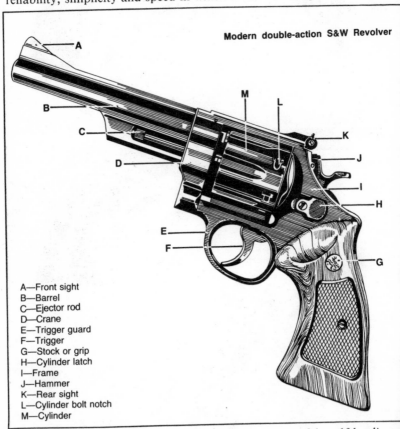

Modern double-action S&W Revolver

A—Front sight
B—Barrel
C—Ejector rod
D—Crane
E—Trigger guard
F—Trigger
G—Stock or grip
H—Cylinder latch
I—Frame
J—Hammer
K—Rear sight
L—Cylinder bolt notch
M—Cylinder

The final handgun development was the invention of the self-loading or semi-automatic pistol. Unlike the revolver, which relies upon the mechanical operation of pulling the trigger to operate it, these firearms used the recoil generated by the firing of a round to reload them. The first reliable semi-automatic pistol was probably the German 'broomhandle' Mauser. This was followed by the famous German 9 mm Parabellum Luger, which was introduced into the German army in 1908.

In 1911, resulting from the ballistic tests already mentioned, the United States Army adopted a semi-automatic pistol in .45 caliber that was designed by John M. Browning and manufactured by Colt. This handgun which rivals the single action Peacemaker revolver in popularity, is one of the most reliable handguns ever made and has formed a basis on which many subsequent self-loading pistols have been designed.

Semi-automatics of this design carry their ammunition in a spring-loaded magazine which is inserted into the bottom of the weapon's handle or butt. With the exception of the barrel, the top portion of the handgun, called the slide, moves backwards and forwards on rails. When the slide is pulled fully to the rear, the magazine spring forces the top-most cartridge up so that its rim is caught by the bottom of the slide as it moves forward. This

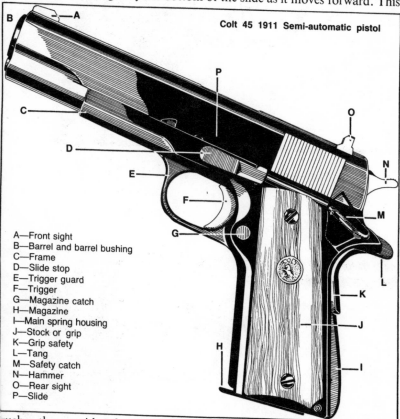

Colt 45 1911 Semi-automatic pistol

A—Front sight
B—Barrel and barrel bushing
C—Frame
D—Slide stop
E—Trigger guard
F—Trigger
G—Magazine catch
H—Magazine
I—Main spring housing
J—Stock or grip
K—Grip safety
L—Tang
M—Safety catch
N—Hammer
O—Rear sight
P—Slide

pushes the cartridge forward into the breach of the barrel. When pulling back the slide it also cocks the hammer back to engage the trigger. On firing, the forces generated by driving the bullet down the barrel cause the slide to move back, withdrawing the empty case and ejecting it, re-cocking the hammer and reloading a fresh round on the forward movement. This will continue every time the trigger is pulled until all rounds have been fired. The most popular descriptive term for self-loading or semi-

Hammerless pocket Automatic

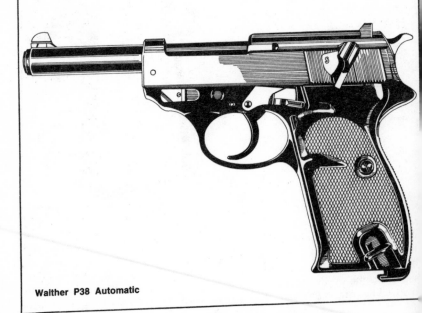

Walther P38 Automatic

20

automatics is just 'automatic'. While the term is, strictly speaking, incorrect (automatic weapons fire continuously until empty as long as the trigger is pulled back), it will be used to describe these handguns throughout the remainder of this book.

Quite popular are the large variety of small hammerless (they do not have an exposed hammer at the back) pocket automatics. These are usually made in calibers of 9 mm and less and are designed to be carried in the pocket.

All of the automatics that have been described, are of the single action variety. Like the revolver they can fire only if the hammer is fully cocked to the rear. With a few exceptions, the Colt .45 Automatic being one, these handguns are unsafe to carry cocked with a round in the chamber. In 1929 the German company of Carl Walther produced the first double action automatic and they followed this just before the war with their famous P 38 pistol in 9 mm that was adopted by the German Army. Like a double action revolver, the trigger of these pistols raises the hammer when pulled back. This allows the gun to be safely carried fully loaded with the hammer down. After the first shot has been fired double action, the remaining rounds are shot single action.

Double action automatics have become quite popular since the Second World War and a number of different makes are now being produced, particularly in Europe. The safest are those that permit the hammer to be lowered by applying the safety catch which can also be placed on safe throughout the loading and unloading procedure. There are some which have a double action trigger but require the hammer to be lowered by hand from the cocked position.

In addition to the advances in handgun and bullet design that have been described, improvements in the metals used have allowed for much more powerful ammunition to be chambered in some guns. In recent years greater use of light alloy metals has been made to conserve weight, although this is not always as desirable as might be thought. To prevent the danger of rusting, a number of revolvers have also been made in stainless steel. Apart from this, there has been little radical change in the design of revolvers and automatics since the Second World War and those available today have been well and truly tried and tested.

Chapter Three

CHOOSING A HANDGUN

Such a wide variety of pistols is on the market today that choosing the right handgun for one's needs is no simple task. The majority of people who buy handguns want one for self-defense but, unfortunately, many end up with a weapon quite unsuited for this purpose. Of those who have made the right choice a large percentage are shooting enthusiasts who usually go to any length to get what they want. As good handguns are becoming very expensive, it is desirable to choose the right one first time, particularly if it is wanted as a means of protection.

In deciding which type of handgun to get for self-defense, a choice has to be made between a revolver or an automatic. As to which of these handguns is the best for this purpose is a constant source of debate between experts and enthusiasts who favour one over the other for a variety of reasons. To listen to all the arguments that have been put forward in support of revolvers or automatics can be very confusing to those who have only a limited knowledge of firearms. It is also rather pointless as, when the pros and cons of each type of handgun are looked at dispassionately, there is very little to choose between them. In the end, personal preferences probably influence most experts and enthusiasts in their final choice of a handgun.

Enthusiasts will invariably find ways and means of reducing any disadvantages their weapons may possess, either by training or modifying the handguns. As the amount of practice of the average gun owner will probably be considerably less, there are a number of factors they must consider when choosing a handgun. These do not necessarily apply to experts and enthusiasts.

In selecting a handgun, one needs to adopt a rational approach, taking into account all the advantages and disadvantages of each type of weapon. These must be weighed against one's own personal circumstances and needs. A comparison between revolvers and automatics reveals that they have the following advantages and disadvantages:—

Double Action Revolvers

Advantages

1. Simple to load and unload.
2. Safe to carry fully loaded.
3. Very reliable. Not rendered inoperable by defective ammunition.
4. Can handle very powerful ammunition.
5. Simple and quick to get into action.

Disadvantages

1. Limited cartridge capacity (5 or 6 rounds).
2. Slow to reload, unless speed loaders are used.
3. Grips not always comfortable to hold.
4. Slightly more difficult to learn to shoot.

Single Action Automatics

Advantages

1. Large cartridge capacity (8 to 18).
2. Can be reloaded quickly if spare full magazine available.
3. Usually has comfortable grips.
4. Compact and easy to conceal.
5. Easier to learn to shoot.

Disadvantages

1. More complicated to load and unload.
2. Unsafe to carry loaded ready for immediate use except in the hands of a well-trained shooter.
3. More prone to malfunctions if dirty or poor grade ammunition is used.

Double Action Automatics

The double action automatic referred to is the type equipped with a safety which, when applied, lowers the hammer without firing it. These have the following additional advantages and disadvantages.

Advantages

1. Safe to carry fully loaded.
2. Safer to operate than single actions because safety can be applied before loading and unloading.

Disadvantages

1. Slightly more difficult to fire first round.

These advantages and detractions must be matched against the following considerations.

Price

The price tag on a handgun is probably the most important consideration in most people's eyes. Good handguns do not come cheaply but, *if you are going to stake your life on one, it is better to pay a little more and get a well-made, reliable weapon.* A good revolver or automatic will last a lifetime, while a cheap one may fail just when you need it most. It is possible to obtain a good secondhand pistol but, unless you know what you are about, you could end up with a lemon.

Safety

One of the most important considerations is obtaining a handgun that you can handle safely, taking into account how much practice you will be able to do. Regular training on the shooting range means you can consider one of the more sophisticated handguns like a single action automatic. On the other hand, *if your practice will be minimal, then choose the simplest, safest weapon you can lay your hands on* like a good double action revolver. These handguns are easy and simple to load and unload while the long double action pull permits them to be carried safely with a fully loaded cylinder. They are in fact, almost completely foolproof and, without intending any disrespect, their simplicity is one of the main reasons why they have been the favourite choice of many police departments for so long.

The medium and small frame revolvers are a good choice for women who can learn to handle them safely in a very much shorter time than it would take with an automatic. In spite of the fact that revolvers are more difficult to learn to shoot, women learn to master the long double action pull in a surprisingly short time.

The single action revolvers are not really suitable as defense weapons, being slow to shoot after the first shot. Loading takes longer and they are not as simple nor as safe as a double action. They should be considered only as a 'fun' gun and suitable for the enthusiast.

The safest automatic is the double action, provided it has a safetycatch that, when applied, lowers the hammer without firing. Although, like all automatics, loading and unloading is more complicated, it is safer with these handguns because the safetycatch can be applied beforehand. Like a revolver, they can be safely carried fully loaded, provided the hammer is at rest. Some authorities argue that these pistols are hard to shoot because of having to change from double to single action after the first shot. This has been rather overplayed and, like the double action revolver, can be mastered with practice. The fact that a number of police forces, as well as some armies, have adopted them should be proof enough of their being a worthwhile proposition for defense.

In the past, single action automatics were considered dangerous to carry with a round in the chamber and cocked ready for use. This certainly applies to most of these automatics and to the small pocket pistols in particular. In recent years there has been growing support for certain of these automatics that have efficient safety catches as being the ultimate in defense handguns when carried 'cocked and locked' (fully loaded, round in chamber, hammer cocked and safety applied).

Without in any way detracting from the merits of these pistols, it must be stressed that a considerable amount of practice is needed if it is intended to carry them on one's person in this condition. During the 1977 World Practical Pistol Championships that were held in Rhodesia, two seasoned competitors had accidental discharges during one stage of the tournament and I personally know one outstanding pistol shot who accidently shot himself in the hand in training. These examples are quoted simply to illustrate the fact that *the carrying of cocked and locked automatics is for experts, not novices.*

Being ready for immediate action is only really necessary if the gun is to be carried on one's person. Guns used for home protection do not have to be stored cocked and locked as there is usually sufficient time to get a round in the chamber. If a smaller automatic has to be carried, it should have the magazine inserted but chamber empty. This is the safest way of carrying

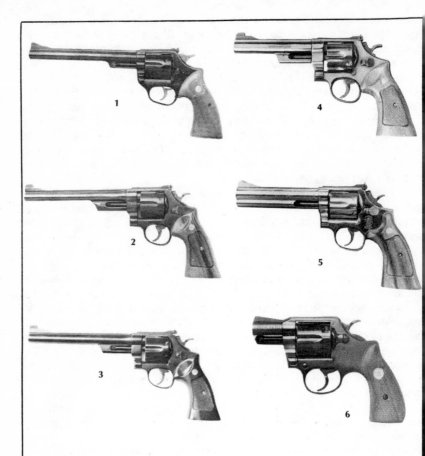

Handguns Suitable for Defense

Large Frame
Double-Action Revolvers

1. ASTRA
Caliber: .357 Magnum, .41 Magnum, .44 Magnum, .45 ACP and .45 Colt. 6 shot cylinder.
Barrel lengths: 3, 4, 6, 8½ inches.
Sights: Rear sight fully adjustable.
Finish: Blue or stainless.

2. SMITH & WESSON Model 29 & 629.
*Caliber: 44 Magnum. 6 shot cylinder.
Barrel lengths: 6 inches Stainless. 4, 6, 8 3/8 inches Blue.
Sights: Rear sight fully adjustable.
Finish: Blue or nickel Model 29. Stainless Model 629.
* Also made in .41 Magnum and known as Model 57.

3. SMITH & WESSON Model 27 & 28.
Caliber: .357 Magnum. 6 shot cylinder.
Barrel lengths: 4, 6, & 8 3/8 inches Model 27. 4 & 6 inches Model 28.
Sights: Rear sight fully adjustable.
Finish: Bright blue & nickel Model 27. Blue only Model 28.

4. SMITH & WESSON Model 25.
Caliber: 45 Colt and .45 ACP. 6 shot cylinder.
Barrel lengths: 6 inches 45 ACP. 4, 6, & 8 3/8 inches ,45 Colt.
Sights: Rear sight fully adjustable.
Finish: Blue

5. SMITH & WESSON Model 581/681 & 586/686.
Caliber: .357 Magnum. 6 shot cylinder.
Barrel lengths: 4 inches 581/681. 4 & 6 inches 586/686.
Sights: Fixed 581/681. Rear sight fully adjustable 586/686.
Finish: Blue, nickel or stainless.

Medium Frame
Double-Action Revolvers

6. COLT LAWMAN.
Caliber: .357 Magnum. 6 shot cylinder.
Barrel lengths: 2 & 4 inches.
Sights: Fixed.
Finish: Blue, nickel and Coltguard.

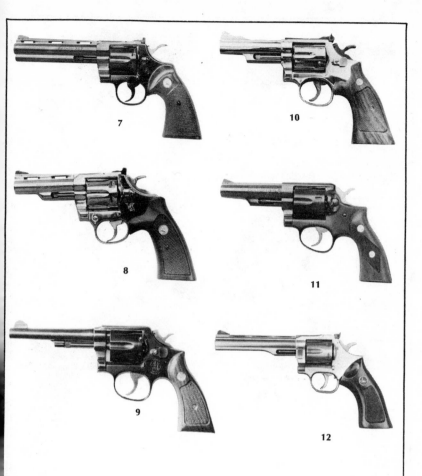

7. COLT PYTHON.
Caliber: .357 Magnum. 6 shot cylinder.
Barrel lenghts: 2½, 4, 6 & 8 inches.
Sights: Rear sight fully adjustable.
Finish: Blue, nickel, Coltguard and stainless.

8. COLT TROOPER.
Caliber: .357 Magnum, .22 LR & .22 WMR.
6 shot cylinder.
Barrel lengths: 4, 6 & 8 inches.
Sights: Rear sight fully adjustable.
Finish: Blue, nickel and Coltguard.

9. SMITH & WESSON Model 10, 13, 64 & 65.
*Caliber: .38 Special Model 10 & 64. .357 Magnum
Model 13 & 65. 6 shot cylinder.
Barrel lengths: 2, 3, 4, 5 & 6 inches.
Sights: Fixed.
Finish: Blue & Nickel - Models 10 & 13
Stainless - Models 54 & 65
* Models 15 (Blue) and 67 (Stainless) similar except
for adjustable sights.

10. SMITH & WESSON Model 19 & 66.
Caliber: .357 Magnum. 6 shot cylinder.
Barrel lengths: 2½, 4, & 6 inches.
Sights: Rear sight fully adjustable.
Finish: Blue & nickel Model 19. Stainless Model 66.

11. STRUM RUGER SPEED-SIX, SECURITY-SIX &
POLICE SERVICE-SIX
Caliber: .357 Magnum. All models. Police Service-
Six also available in 9 mm. 6 Shot cylinder.
Barrel lengths: 2¾, 4 & 6 inches Security-Six. 2¾ &
4 inches other models.
Sights: Rear sight fully adjustable on Security-Six.
Other models have fixed sights.
Finish: Blue & stainless.

12. DAN WESSON Model 14-2, 15-2 & 715.
Caliber: .357 Magnum. 6 shot cylinder.
Barrel lengths: Interchangable varying from 2½ to
15 inches.
Sights: Fixed Model 14-2, rear sight fully adjustable
Model 15-2 & 715.
Finish: Blue Model 14-2 & 15-2. Stainless Model 715

Small Frame
Double-Action Revolvers

13. CHARTER ARMS BULLDOG & UNDERCOVER.
Caliber: .44 Special Bulldog and Target Bulldog.
5 shot cylinder. 357 Magnum Target Bulldog
& Tracker. 5 shot cylinder. .38 Special Police
Bulldog. 6 shot cylinder. .38 Special and .32
S&W Long Undercover. 5 & 6 shot cylinder.
Barrel lengths: Between 2 & 6 inches, depending on
model.
Sights: Fixed Bulldog & Undercover. Rear sight fully
adjustable other models.
Finish: Most models available in blue and stainless.

14. COLT DETECTIVE SPECIAL & AGENT.
Caliber: .38 Special.
Barrel length: 6 shot cylinder. 2.
Sights: Fixed.
Finish: Blue & nickel Detective Special. Parkerized
Agent. Agent has alloy frame.

15. COLT DIAMONDBACK.
Caliber: .38 Special & .22LR. 6 shot cylinder.
Barrel length: 4 & 6 inches.
Sights: Rear sight fully adjustable.
Finish: Blue & nickel.

16. SMITH & WESSON Model 31, 36, 37 & 60.
Caliber: .32 S&W Long Model 31. .38 Special
Model 36, 37 & 60. 5 shot cylinder.
Barrel length: 2 & 3 inches.
Sights: Fixed.
Finish: Blue Model 31, Blue & nickel Model 36 & 37
(Alloy Frame) Stainless Model 60.

17. SMITH & WESSON Model 38 & 49.
Caliber: .38 Special. 5 shot cylinder.
Barrel length: 2 inches.
Sights: Fixed.
Finish: Blue & nickel. Model 38 Alloy Frame.

Large
Double-Action Automatics.

18. ASTRA A-80.
Caliber: 9 mm & .38 Super (15 Shot). .45 ACP
(9 Shot).
Barrel length: 4 inches.
Sights: Fixed.
Finish: Blue.

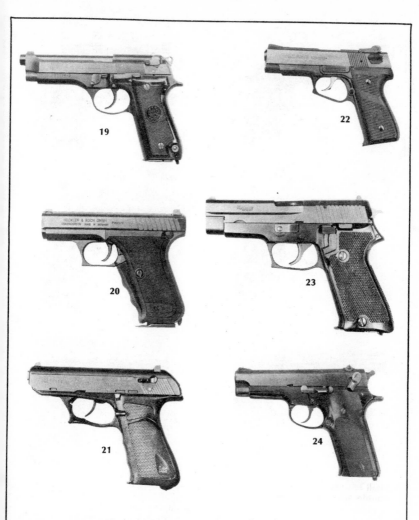

19. BERETTA MODEL 92S & 92SB COMPACT.
Caliber: 9 mm. 15 Shot (92S). 13 Shot (92SB).
Barrel length: 5 inches.
Sights: Fixed.
Finish: Blue.

20. HECKLER & KOCH P7.
Caliber: 9 mm. 8 Shot.
Barrel length: 4 inches.
Sights: Fixed.
Finish: Blue.
Utilizes unique squeeze cocking lever to cock the
    action.

21. HECKLER & KOCK P9S.
Caliber: 9 mm. 9 Shot. .45 ACP 7 Shot.
Barrel length: 4 inches.
Sights: Fixed.
Finish: Blue.

22. LLAMA OMNI.
Caliber: 9 mm. 13 Shot. .45 ACP 7 Shot.
Barrel length: 4 inches.
Sights: Fully adjustable rear sight.
Finish: Blue.

23. SIG/SAUER M220 & M225.
Caliber: 9 mm. .38 Super 9 Shot & .45 ACP 7 Shot
    M220. 9 mm. 9 Shot M225.
Barrel length: 4.4 inches M220. 3.8 inches M225.
Sights: Fixed.
Finish: Blue.

24. SMITH & WESSON MODELS 439, 539, 639 &
    459, 559, 659.
Caliber: 9 mm. 8 Shot (439, 539, 639) 14 Shot (459,
    559, 659).
Barrel length: 4 inches.
Sights: Rear sight fully adjustable.
Finish: Blue & nickel 439, 539, 459, 559. Stainless
    639, 659. (439 & 459 have alloy frames).

25. STAR Model 28
Caliber: 9 mm. 15 Shot.
Barrel length: 4.33 inches.
Sights: Rear sight adjustable for windage only.
Finish: Blue.

26. WALTHER P5.
Caliber: 9 mm. 8 Shot.
Barrel length: 3.5 inches.
Sights: Rear adjustable for windage only.
Finish: Blue.

27. WALTHER P-38.
Caliber: 9 mm. 8 Shot.
Barrel length: 5 inches.
Sights: Fixed.
Finish: Blue.

Small
Double-Action Automatics

28. BERETTA 81 & 84.
Caliber: .32 12 Shot & .380 ACP 13 Shot.
Barrel length: 3¾ inches.
Sights: Fixed.
Finish: Blue.

29. HECKLER·& KOCH HK-4.
Caliber: .22 LR, .25, .32 8 Shot. .380 7 Shot.
Barrel length: 3 11/32 inches.
Sights: Fixed.
Finish: Blue. Available with conversion kit for all
        calibers.

30. SIG/SAUER M230.
Caliber: .380 7 Shot.
Barrel length: 3.6 inches.
Sights: Fixed.
Finish: Blue.

31. SMITH & WESSON Model 469.
Caliber: 9 mm. 13 Shot.
Barrel length: 3.5 inches.
Sights: Fixed.
Finish: Blue.

32. WALTHER MODEL PP & PPK.
Caliber: .22 LR 10 Shot, .32 8 Shot, .380 7 Shot Model PP .380 7 Shot Model PPK.
Barrel length: 3 7/8 inches Model PP. 3 1/4 inches Model PPK.
Sights: Fixed.
Finish: Blue.

Large
Single-Action Automatics.

33. BROWNING HI-POWER.
Caliber: 9 mm. 14 Shot;
Barrel length: 4¾ inches.
Sights: Available with fixed and fully adjustable rear sight.
Finish: Blue, nickel and silver chrome.

34. COLT GOVERNMENT MODEL, ACE,
GOLD CUP, COMMANDER.
Caliber: .22LR 10 Shot (Ace), 45 ACP 7 Shot (Gov. Model & Gold Cup), .38 Super & 9 mm. 9 Shot (Gov. Model).

Barrel length: 5 inches.
Sights: Fixed Gov. Model. Rear sight fully adjustable Ace & Gold Cup.
Finish: Blue, nickel Gov. Model. Blue Ace & Gold Cup. Commander and Combat Commander versions same in all respects to the Gov. Model except for shortened barrel (4¼ inches) and slide and burr hammer.

Small
Single-Action Automatics

35. AMT BACKUP.
Caliber: .22 LR 8 Shot. .380 5 Shot.
Barrel length: 2¼ inches.
Sights: Fixed.
Finish: Stainless.

36. STAR MODELS PD, BK & BKM.
Caliber: .45 ACP 6 Shot (PD), 9 mm. 9 Shot (BK & BKM)
Barrel lengths: 3½ inches (PD), 4¼ inches (BK & BKM)
Sights: Rear sight fully adjustable (PD) Fixed (BK & BKM)
Finish: Blue. PD & BKM have alloy frames.

these handguns and can be used even for those automatics that may be carried cocked and locked because a round can be loaded into the chamber very quickly.

Caliber

The arguments as to which caliber is the best for defense work is probably even more controversial than the revolver vs automatic debate. For defense, a bullet that will effectively stop an attacker in his tracks is what is sought and there is little argument that calibers of .41 and above will all do this admirably. The problem is that the handguns chambered for these big calibers are invariably large, heavy and difficult to control when fired quickly. One of the best compromises in knockdown power and controllability is the Colt .45 Government automatic which also has one of the best safety systems for carrying cocked and locked. While the large caliber handguns are potentially the best defense weapons, a lot of practice is needed to learn to shoot them quickly and accurately. The ammunition they digest is also expensive with the result that most dedicated shooters reload (manufacture fresh ammunition using empty cartridge cases) in order to economize. For these reasons, they are not suitable for everyone.

There is wide agreement on the minimum calibers suitable for defense. For revolvers, nothing smaller than 38 Special and automatics, 9 mm parabellum, should be considered. It is also possible to get revolvers that are chambered for the powerful 357 Magnum round, an excellent manstopper, which also chambers 38 Special without difficulty. While not as effective as the larger calibers, handguns chambered for either of these rounds can be considered suitable for defense. Ammunition is readily available and usually reasonably priced while the handguns are easy to shoot. Women are often encouraged to buy pistols in smaller calibers in the mistaken belief that a 38 or 9 mm is too big for them to handle. Nothing could be further from the truth as women can learn to shoot automatics or revolvers chambered for either round as well as some of the bigger calibers. While the smaller calibers can be lethal, they very often will not stop an attacker unless a vital organ is hit.

Reliability

For a handgun to fail just when it is needed to ward off an attack can be disastrous, particularly as this is most likely to occur at close range. Provided they are in mechanically sound working order, handguns usually fail to function because of dirt or defective ammunition. One of the greatest assets of revolvers is their ability to continue shooting even if a round fails to fire.

The failure rate of modern automatics has been very much reduced, due mainly to improved design and manufacture of handguns and ammunition. In spite of this improvement, they are still more prone to malfunction. If chosen as a defense weapon, care in cleaning and selection of ammunition is essential if stoppages are to be avoided. It is also strongly recommended that clearing of malfunctions should be a regular feature of training.

Size and Weight

Contrary to popular belief, small handguns are not easy to shoot even though they are often chosen as defense weapons. The small pocket automatics are very difficult to handle and shoot, especially for women. They have very hard trigger pulls and stiff, small safety and magazine catches that are difficult to operate, while the small grips and poor sights do little to aid good shooting. Both men and women are better off with bigger guns which are, in fact, easier to hold and fire.

There are really only two considerations regarding size and weight. Most important is getting a gun you can hold comfortably and, at the same time, engage the trigger correctly with the index finger. If the gun is too big you will have difficulty in doing this but the medium frame handguns usually suit most people. Weight, provided the gun is not *too* heavy, is an advantage and helps make the gun more controllable during rapid shooting.

Size and weight can be an important consideration if the gun is to be carried on one's person. Once again the common belief is that small lightweight handguns are the only choice as a holster gun. In fact, provided you have a good holster and belt, most medium-sized pistols can be carried quite comfortably and concealed, if necessary.

As regards barrel length, particularily of revolvers, it is often believed that those revolvers with two-inch (50 mm) barrels are ideal for carrying concealed. In fact the short barrel makes these guns difficult to holster and very hard to control in rapid fire. Their main value is their ability to be carried in the pocket or handbag, in which case the light-weight models should be chosen. In revolvers, the most popular barrel length is four inches (100 mm) which holster well, even when concealed, is long enough to provide accuracy when shooting fast, and is not detrimental to the velocity of the bullet. Revolvers with long barrels (six inches (150 mm) being the most popular) are more accurate because of the greater distance between the sights but not so easy to conceal if they have to be carried.

What has just been said applies mainly to revolvers. Automatics are more compact and easier to carry concealed, even in the big calibers. They also have better grips and are, therefore, more comfortable to hold although the grips of revolvers can be vastly improved by fitting a set of the commercially available custom stocks.

Ammunition Capacity

In the firepower department, automatics have a decided edge over revolvers. They carry more ammunition and can be reloaded more quickly if a spare full magazine is available. The cylinder capacity of revolvers is either five or six rounds while the large automatics hold anything from eight to 15 or more. The loading of revolvers can be speeded up by using quick or speed loaders (devices that insert five or six rounds into the chamber simultaneously), but this is still not as fast as a magazine change with an automatic.

These advantages are lauded by those who favour the automatic, but just how desirable a large magazine capacity and an ability to reload really is, is debatable. Police records throughout the world show that most shootings are decided on average, after some three rounds have been fired. This tends to indicate that the advantage of being able to reload quickly is not such an important consideration as many believe.

For the average person who wants a handgun for personal or home defense a large ammunition capacity is not essential although it is obviously something that is nice to have. Automatic pistols with large magazine capacities are really intended for military or specialized police units. Here firepower is important and a handgun that has the ability to fire a large number of rounds before the need to reload has a definite advantage.

Sights and Triggers

Sights and trigger pull should always be considered when choosing a handgun. Good sights enable the gun to be aimed correctly, which is vital to accurate shooting, while trigger pull can disturb the sight alignment if it is too stiff. (These aspects are covered in greater detail in Chapter 10 'Accessories and Modifications').

Single action automatics are generally easier to shoot because only a relatively light pressure on the trigger is needed to fire them. Although also able to fire single action, double action revolvers and automatics are not so easy to shoot because of the long heavy trigger pull needed to raise the hammer. Ironically the top grade revolvers usually have the best triggers (both double and single action) and sights of all handguns.

When considering the trigger pull of a single action, it must not be too stiff or have too much drag before the hammer is released. A double action pull, while heavier, should not be too stiff and must be relatively smooth.

Handgun sights, when viewed from the rear should be large and easy to pick up quickly with the eyes. If the gun has to be carried in a holster, then the front sight should be rounded or ramped. The majority of defense handguns have sights that are an integral part of the gun, although quite a few of the top revolvers are fitted with fully adjustable target sights. These revolvers are not only suitable for defense but many make very good target pistols. It is possible to get automatics with adjustable sights or have them fitted but, if the latter modification is carried out, great care must be taken. Adjustable sights fitted to automatics have a disturbing tendency to shake loose from the continual slamming backwards and forwards of the slide during firing.

The type of handguns used in the sports of Target Pistol Shooting and Practical Pistol Shooting are more fully described in the Chapter 'Pistol Shooting as a Sport'. Nevertheless, as many gunowners often turn to either of these sports because they find shooting their own pistol so enjoyable, it is worth considering what defense handguns can also be used in either of these activities.

The sport of target shooting is very specialized and most of the matches use pistols designed solely for that event. Only in one event, the Center Fire Match, are large caliber handguns used and those revolvers in 38 Special or 357 Magnum with 6-inch (150 mm) barrels and equipped with target sights are used by many shooters with excellent results.

In practical pistol shooting, which is much more closely allied to defensive shooting, the most popular handguns are single action automatics with button magazine release catches in either 9 mm or 45 caliber that can be safely carried cocked and locked. These pistols are often extensively modified to such an extent that they rival the best target handguns in the degree of accuracy they can deliver. Although not popular, there is no reason why some of the double action automatics with button type magazine release catches cannot be used. It is also possible to use a revolver and those suitable for target shooting, preferably in 357 Magnum, would be as good as any. Revolvers are, however, very much handicapped in this sport because of the emphasis placed on fast reloading.

In conclusion, there is probably no perfect defense handgun that will completely satisfy everyone's need. You have to consider all the pros and cons of each handgun and balance these against your own particular circumstances. Some readers will probably already possess a handgun and, after reading this chapter, realize that it does not live up to what they really need. While their best course would obviously be to trade it in for a more suitable handgun, this may not always be possible. If you have such a handgun and decide to keep it, then at least appreciate its shortcomings, and take what steps you can in your practice and training to make the best of what you have.

Chapter Four

FIREARMS RESPONSIBILITY

No one should contemplate owning a handgun unless they are prepared to accept the responsibility that goes with it. Just as a motor vehicle only becomes lethal when driven by an incompetent person, so firearms are only dangerous when they fall into untrained or irresponsible hands. A handgun, in particular, is little use as a means of self-protection unless the owner knows how to handle it safely, can secure it from falling into the hands of criminals or children and is fully acquainted with the law regarding its possession and when it may be lawfully used.

Lawful possession of a handgun is the first responsibility. At the time of this writing, there are federal laws relating to gun ownership as well as state statutes and municipal ordinances. Generally speaking, the federal law requires all retail sales of handguns to be done through a federally licensed firearms dealer who is required to keep accurate records of all sales to private citizens.

Federal laws, of course, apply throughout the country. In addition to this, many states and municipalities have their own laws and ordinances relating to handgun ownership. Depending upon the location, these vary from hardly any restrictions to strict controls where a police permit is required to acquire and possess a pistol or revolver.

Even in those areas that do not restrict private handgun ownership, a permit is often needed if it is desired to carry one concealed on one's person or in a vehicle or even openly exposed. There are, in fact, very few places left that do not have some controls over firearm ownership and it is up to you to find out exactly what your local laws are in this respect. Specific information on such laws and how they apply to you can usually be obtained from your local gunshop or gun clubs.

It is equally important that you be fully aware of when you may use a handgun as a means of self-defense. In this respect it is important to realize that, because most instances when handguns are resorted to for self-defense usually occur at close range in poor light conditions, it is rarely possible to get off an aimed shot. All that you can hope to do is to shoot at the biggest target which will probably be the trunk area of your assailant. Under such circumstances, there is a good chance the bullet will strike a vital area with fatal results.

For this reason any firearm must only be resorted to as a last resort in a life threatening situation. Because the laws relating to the use of lethal force may vary from state to state, it is not possible to cover every possible situation in which a firearm can be used to defend oneself. All that can be done is to lay down some basic principles and strongly recommend that readers take the trouble to acquaint themselves with their local laws relating to this subject.

Most laws recognize the fact that law abiding citizens may have to resort to force to defend themselves when unlawfully attacked. For such force to be deemed justifiable, it must be reasonable. This means that only enough force to overcome or repel the unlawful attack may be used and must cease immediately when the danger is past. In addition, such force is only justifiable when the unlawful attack has either commenced or is imminent. Threats of future harm would not justify the use of force because there is time to make a report to the police.

Because a handgun is the most lethal degree of force one can resort to, its use is only lawful if your life, the lives of your family or other innocent persons are in imminent danger of death or great bodily injury. Where an assault is of such a nature that there is no chance of death or serious injury, shooting would render one liable to criminal as well as civil action. Even in a life threatening situation, a handgun must always be considered as a last resort when there is no other way of repelling or avoiding the unlawful attack. Once the danger is past the shooting must cease immediately. As certain aspects of the laws relating to the lethal force do vary in some states, it is important that you find out what applies to you in the area where you live.

In any potential shooting incident, the lives of innocent persons must also be considered. This is especially so if one has a lawful need to carry a handgun in public. Under such circumstances one must make every effort to avoid engaging in a gun battle in a crowded street because of the danger of innocent bystanders being hit by stray shots. Here it is most important to be able to hit one's intended target quickly and effectively.

Where a handgun is intended for home protection, precautions must be taken to avoid mistakenly shooting a family member. This requires developing a plan of action that can be implemented in the event of there being a suspected intruder in the house. A good plan is to get all family members into the master bedroom if a burglary is suspected before taking any further action. You can then decide whether to investigate or simply guard the family in the bedroom until the police arrive.

The point is, a handgun should never be looked upon as the sole means of protecting the home for, no matter how good a shot you may be, it is of little use if you are caught by surprise or while asleep. A gun is only part of home security and physical protection in the form of well constructed doors, locks and even a burglar alarm system are needed to give you warning and time to get hold of a handgun.

Everyone who owns a handgun has the responsibility to take all reasonable precautions to prevent it from falling into the wrong hands. This is of particular concern to a family which has children who are not old enough to appreciate the dangers associated with firearms. The problem is how to keep the gun secure yet still reasonably accessible in an emergency.

Much depends upon your personal circumstances but, whenever possible, firearms should be kept under lock and key when not needed. There are a number of ways in which a handgun can be secured. The best is a well constructed safe or firearms cabinet, preferably built into a wall or bolted to the floor. There are a number of such safes made especially for handguns that range from large cabinets in which several guns can be secured to small ones that can be installed into a wall and covered by a picture. It is also possible to use a closet, making it more secure by fitting it with a solid core door that has a deadbolt lock.

Being a compact object, another way of securing a handgun is to keep it in a strong steel cash box that has a secure lock. Kept up high in a cupboard or a closet, it will keep children from getting at it but not a determined thief who simply has to remove it and open it later at his leisure. A little more security can be given to the box by drilling holes in its bottom and bolting it to a shelf.

Keeping the gun in a locked cupboard or drawer is the least secure method. While it may be enough to keep it away from small children, these locks are invariably of cheap construction that can be opened with a common key or simply forced open. If the gun is to be kept in such a place, it should be at least fitted with a decent lock.

One way of securing handguns from children is to render them temporarily inoperable. There are trigger lock devices obtainable that fit over the trigger guard of both revolvers and automatics that positively prevent the gun from being fired. Swing-out double-action revolvers can be rendered inoperable by releasing the cylinder and placing a good quality padlock over the topstrap. This effectively prevents the gun from being fired as the cylinder cannot be closed into the frame.

When there is an immediate need for the handgun, such as at night, it can be removed from its place of security to be more readily available. However, it is not recommended that the handgun be kept under a pillow or on a nightstand because of the danger of waking up in a panic and shooting while half-asleep. To avoid mistakenly shooting a family member it is important to be fully awake when taking hold of a handgun in an emergency. A better plan is to have the gun placed on a high shelf which requires you having to get out of bed to get it, by which time you should be fully awake.

Where a loaded handgun is kept readily available in the house at night, there is always a danger of a family member returning home when the others are asleep and being mistaken for a burglar. Such a member should always have to wake up the others to gain entry rather than let themselves in with a key. Any inconvenience caused is well worth the possible tragedy averted.

Where there are children in the house, they should be exposed to the responsibilities of safe handgun handling as soon as possible. Unfortunately, all too often, a handgun is treated as something the children are forbidden to see. All this does is to arouse a natural inquisitiveness that all children have, increasing the likelihood that they will try to get hold of the gun and see what this fascinating thing is all about.

It is better to remove the mystery of a gun in the home and make them aware of what can happen if safety and security measures are ignored as soon as they are old enough to understand. Letting them actually witness a handgun being fired will help them realize its lethal potential better than words can describe. Boys are naturally interested in guns and should be introduced to basic gun manners and safety as soon as possible. Accidents rarely happen to children who have been educated in firearms safety but this does not mean that loaded guns can be left unsecured. While the children of the house may be trustworthy, this does not apply to their friends should they manage to get hold of the gun.

Finally, there are some other points worth considering. Just as drink and driving are taboo, so alcohol and firearms don't mix. Guns have no place in bars, parties or other functions where alcohol is to be consumed. Going armed with a loaded pistol to such a function is asking for trouble. Of course one of the most important responsibilities is being able to handle your handgun safely and this is covered in detail in the next chapter.

Chapter Five

SAFETY FIRST

Safety is such an important, if not the most important, aspect of firearms proficiency that it justifies a chapter all to itself. Accurate shooting is meaningless if you could accidently shoot yourself or, worse still, someone else, because of unsafe handgun handling. For this reason every gun owner, or potential gun owner, has a clear duty to ensure that he, or she, can at least handle guns safely.

The two rules of firearms safety that must be followed are:
1. Treat every gun as being loaded until you have personally checked that it is empty; and,
2. Never point a firearm at anyone or thing you do not intend to shoot.

Develop the habit of always checking any firearm you are given or pick up regardless of what you believe its condition to be.

Many handguns differ in how they are loaded, unloaded and field stripped for cleaning. *Make sure, therefore, that you know exactly how your gun, or the one you intend acquiring, works,* either by reading any instructions that come with it, or getting someone who knows the handgun to show you how it operates.

The first step when picking up any handgun is to *make it safe* by checking to see if it is loaded and, if it is, removing all the cartridges. How you pick up and hold a handgun is very important because its short barrel makes it easy to inadvertently point it at someone.

The correct way to pick up a pistol is to grip it normally in your shooting hand, *but keep your finger away from the trigger* by placing it alongside the frame, making sure the barrel always points in a safe direction.

The simplest handgun to handle is a double action revolver but first make sure that the hammer is down. If the hammer is in fact cocked then it must be lowered before the cylinder can be opened. To do this safely, check

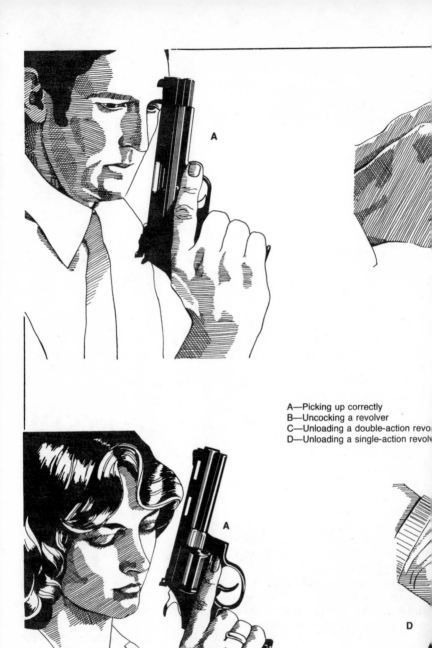

A—Picking up correctly
B—Uncocking a revolver
C—Unloading a double-action revo[lver]
D—Unloading a single-action revol[ver]

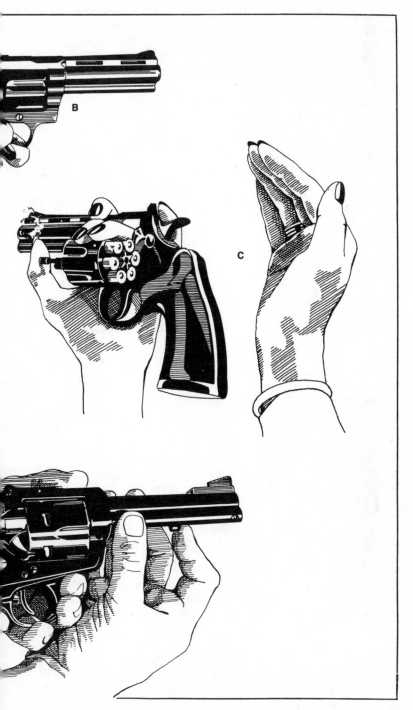

B

C

43

that the barrel points in a safe direction and that your finger is away from the trigger. Then grasp the hammer with the thumb of the free hand, pull it back, then pull the trigger and gently lower the hammer.

To unload a double action revolver first transfer it to the free hand. Then, swing out the cylinder or break the handgun and remove any cartridges with the extractor rod.

Unloading a single action revolver is slightly different. After placing the gun in the free hand, open the loading gate, pull the hammer back to half-cock (unless the gun is a new model Ruger, in which case leave the hammer at rest) and remove the cartridges by using the ejector rod.

Automatics are more complicated to handle and must be dealt with very carefully. Such handguns must be kept in the shooting hand during the entire unloading procedure. Having picked it up as described, apply the safety catch if this is possible. Some automatic safeties can only be applied if the hammer is cocked.

Next remove the magazine. *Be careful with small automatics* which often have stiff, tiny magazine catches. These can be difficult to operate and can cause you to point the barrel in the wrong direction as you struggle to remove the magazine.

Still keeping the fingers away from the trigger and the barrel away from trouble, grasp the slide firmly with the fingers and thumb of the other hand and pull it back to its fullest extent. This will remove any round in the chamber but *always look into the chamber to make sure that it is empty*. A broken or worn extractor or ejector can fail to remove the round from the gun. If you were able to apply the safety after you picked up the gun, you may have to release it in order to operate the slide.

Before loading an automatic or revolver you must first go through the procedure just described to ensure that it is empty. Double action revolvers are very simple to load. Simply insert your cartridges into the chambers of the cylinder and close it. With a good double action you can safely load all chambers, but single actions (unless they have a transfer bar like the new Rugers), *must never be carried with a round under the hammer*. This type of revolver can accidently fire if dropped on the hammer when loaded in this condition.

To load an automatic, insert a loaded magazine into the grip, making sure that you push it fully home. If your pistol is one that permits loading and unloading with the safety on, it should be applied. The slide is then pulled back to its fullest extent and released. Allow it to go forward un-assisted, ensuring that it is fully home before you apply the safety catch.

These safety procedures can be quite easily practised in the home with an unloaded pistol, so get that gun down from its dusty shelf, find out how it works, and start practising. There is no excuse for unsafe handgun handling. *If you are not prepared to become a safe shooter, you should not possess a firearm.*

Clearing Stoppages

At some stage — hopefully only when you are practising — your pistol may fail to fire. In the majority of instances this will most likely be due to dirt or

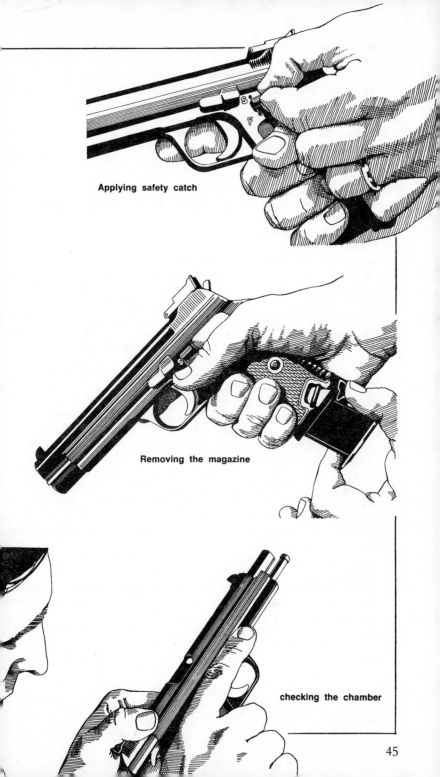

Applying safety catch

Removing the magazine

checking the chamber

45

defective ammunition unless some vital part of the pistol is damaged or broken. Stoppages due to dirt or poor ammunition can be easily cleared unless, due to only the primer igniting, a bullet is stuck in the barrel. Such a stoppage may need the services of a gunsmith but, fortunately, is very rare.

Malfunctions due to ammunition failure in revolvers rarely present any problems, unless a bullet is lodged in the barrel. Just pull the trigger again and fire the next round. Stoppages in automatics are not so simple to deal with. Poor ammunition can fail to generate enough recoil to eject completely a spent case or feed the next round, although it might also be due to a dirty gun. Failure of a cartridge to fire is a very common cause of malfunctions and, while not so frequent, inadvertently touching the button type of magazine release catch during firing, thereby releasing it, can be another reason. To prevent ammunition failure, *only fresh ammunition* should be loaded. Old ammunition should be used for practice.

The most positive method of clearing stoppages in automatics is first to remove the magazine. Then pull back the slide to eject the defective round or spent case. Replace the magazine, making sure it is fully home, then pull back the slide to chamber a fresh round, putting the gun back into action. If a round has failed to fire, you can simply pull back the slide but, if the malfunction is for any other cause, this may not work. Although malfunctions are rare in a well-made automatic that is kept clean and fed good ammunition, practice in clearing malfunctions quickly is strongly recommended.

Safety On The Range

There are certain very important safety rules that apply at any place where live ammunition is to be expended. Some ranges have their own procedures, but the following have almost universal application.

1. Load and unload only when on the firing point and after permission to do so has been given.
2. Keep the muzzle of the handgun pointed in the direction of the target at all times. Never turn round with the pistol in your hand.
3. Shoot only after the command to fire has been given and stop immediately if ordered to cease fire.
4. Do not leave the firing point or go forward to examine your target without permission.
5. Have the cylinder of your revolver or the slide of your automatic open or locked back after the command 'Cease fire, Unload' has been given. This assists the Range Officer in checking that all guns are safe.
6. Never touch or handle your handgun on the firing point when others are forward changing targets.
7. Unload and make your handgun safe before leaving the firing point.

Ear Protection

In recent years the harmful effects of excessive noise have been very much in the news and it is now an established fact that constant exposure to the noise generated by the muzzle-blast of firearms can cause permanent damage to hearing.

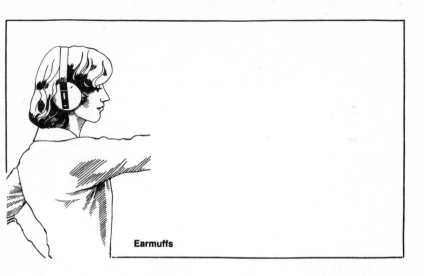

Earmuffs

Ear protection in the form of muffs or plugs can be obtained at gun-shops and are not expensive. Ear muffs are the most popular, being easy and comfortable to wear. Ear plugs, to be effective, must be inserted into the ear channel correctly. While they are effective they can become uncomfortable after a time. Although not as effective, moist cotton wool inserted in the ear channel will give some protection and is better than nothing at all.

Even if you intend to do only enough shooting to achieve a sufficient degree of pistol proficiency for self-protection it pays to invest in a set of ear muffs. Apart from protecting your hearing, you will not have to put up with the discomfort of hearing the loud reports made by your guns and those of others. By blocking out most of this noise you will find it far easier to shoot effectively.

Chapter Six

THE PRINCIPLES OF PISTOL SHOOTING

When analysed, all that accurate shooting with any firearm (except perhaps shotguns) consists of is *aiming the firearm correctly at the target and firing without disturbing the alignment of the sights on the target*. In pistol shooting, these two principles are *vital* to accurate shooting because, of all the firearms, handguns are the most difficult to shoot. They can be supported only by the hands and, because of the short distance between the front and rear sights (called sight radius) any error in aiming or pulling the trigger is greatly magnified. Although many modern handguns are quite capable of shooting accurately over considerable distances, it is the difficulty experienced in firing them that makes them inferior to shoulder weapons for long range work.

Correct sight alignment and trigger control are, therefore, the two most important principles of pistol shooting that apply regardless of whether the shooter is engaged in target shooting or using a handgun to repel an unlawful attack. The difference is confined to the methods used to apply these principles. In target shooting, one is restricted to using an upright stance and only one hand to grip, aim and fire the pistol. Such restrictions do not usually apply to defense or the sport of practical pistol shooting where two hands may be used to grip the handgun as well as a variety of shooting positions that can be adopted for different situations.

A good grip on the pistol together with a firm shooting stance will greatly assist in aiming and firing the pistol. The best methods of holding and standing will, therefore, be described first before going on to deal with aiming and trigger control.

Gripping or Holding the Pistol

The first step towards accurate pistol shooting is to hold the handgun correctly. Ideally, the grip should point the pistol naturally towards the target, be firm enough to prevent movement in the hand during recoil and position the index finger (trigger finger) so that the pull on the trigger is applied *directly to the rear*.

How the trigger finger engages the trigger is very important. To avoid pulling the pistol off the point of aim the index finger must engage the trigger with either the *first pad or joint* making sure that no part of the frame or trigger guard is touched. The direction of the pull must be directly to the rear.

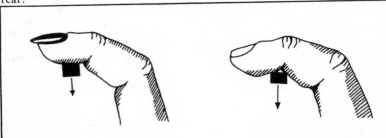

Spend some time experimenting with your pistol to obtain the grip that suits you best. This can be done by carefully fitting the handgun into the shooting hand and adjusting your grip until you are able to hold it correctly yet comfortable. To do this, pick up your unloaded pistol in the free hand

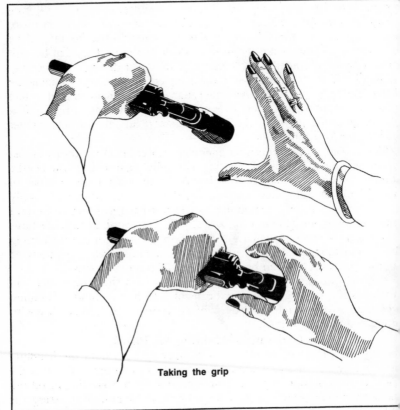

Taking the grip

and spread the index finger and the thumb of the shooting hand apart to form a V.

Fit the gun into the shooting hand making sure that the web of the shooting hand formed by the V is positioned high on the pistol's backstrap. With a double action revolver fit the web of your hand just under the little hump at the top of the back of the grip. With automatics it should be placed well into the curved tang of the frame.

Correct placement of the thumb assists in controlling recoil and helps in trigger control. When shooting a revolver single action the thumb is placed high, either parallel to the trigger finger or resting alongside the frame. If the latter method is used be careful not to press against the hammer as this may cause misfires.

For double action revolver shooting the thumb is locked tightly down in order to obtain maximum control of the long trigger pull and to prevent the gun moving in the hand during recoil.

With automatics, regardless of whether they are single or double action, the thumb is also placed high alongside the frame almost parallel to the trigger finger.

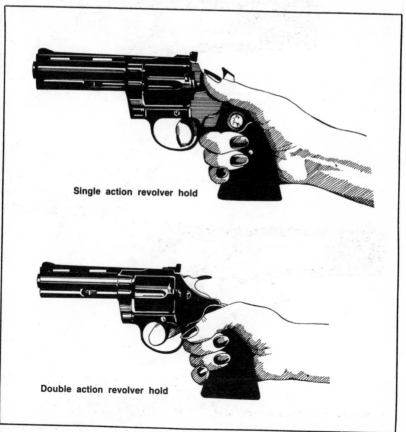

Single action revolver hold

Double action revolver hold

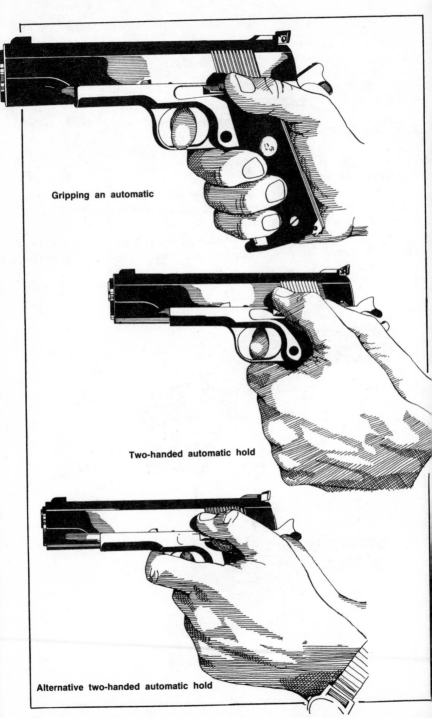

Gripping an automatic

Two-handed automatic hold

Alternative two-handed automatic hold

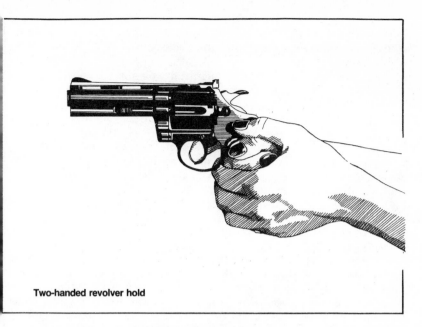

Two-handed revolver hold

The grip of a top shooter on his pistol is like a vice so your hold must be as tight as possible without inducing shake or tremor. To achieve this, try gripping the gun as tightly as you can until your hand shakes, then, gradually relax your hold until the shaking stops at which point your grip will be firm enough.

What has just been described is the method of gripping a pistol for

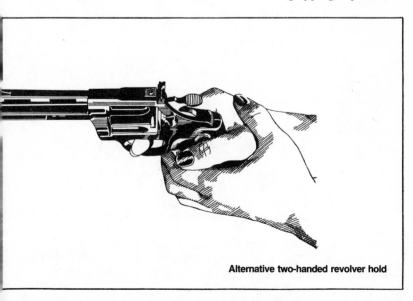

Alternative two-handed revolver hold

one-handed shooting. When two hands are used the grip of the shooting hand does not change but is simply given additional support by the other. With a revolver the fingers of the free hand are cupped over those gripping the butt. There are two ways of placing the thumb of the supporting hand. One method is to place it over the thumb of the shooting hand.

The other method is to place the thumb across the back of the shooting hand. This has the advantage of permitting quick cocking of the revolver with the thumb of the free hand if single action fire is desired.

When using two hands to grip an automatic simply wrap the fingers of the supporting hand around the hand gripping the pistol. The fingers of the supporting hand should form a platform under the trigger guard while the thumb is placed either over or alongside the other one. *DO NOT PLACE THE THUMB ACROSS THE BACK OF THE SHOOTING HAND AS IN GRIPPING A REVOLVER AS IT CAN BE INJURED BY EITHER THE HAMMER OR THE SLIDE AS THEY MOVE BACK-WARDS AFTER FIRING.*

Some shooters like to curl the index finger of the supporting hand around the front of the trigger guard maintaining this assists in controlling the recoil of the handgun. The drawback of this method is that there may be a tendency to pull the pistol down when firing. It can also take a little longer to assume when the pistol is drawn from the holster in a hurry.

Many muscles in the hand and arm that are not normally used come into play when a shooting a pistol. These will develop with regular pistol practice but can also be strengthened by exercising with either grip-exercisers or compressing an old tennis ball in the hand. In time you will find that you can pick up your handgun and hold it correctly without having to make any adjustments.

The Stance

As most pistol shooting is done from an upright stance, your posture when shooting a pistol is most important. A good stance will reduce body movement to a minimum and assist in holding the pistol steady when aiming. A bad stance, on the other hand, will increase muscular tension and body movement.

To assume a good stance, for target or defence shooting, you should stand upright but relaxed with your body weight evenly distributed through the balls of both feet.

The one-handed shooting stance will be dealt with first. This is the stance which is used mainly by target shooters although it is also needed on occasions in defence shooting as well. Position your feet apart, the distance between the heels roughly about the width of your shoulders, and angled about 45 degrees to the line of fire.

The arm holding the pistol is held straight with the elbow locked while the free hand is either placed in the trouser pocket or on the hip. The body and head are held erect with the eyes aligning the sights with the target.

In defence shooting the two-handed hold on the pistol should be used whenever possible and there are two stances to choose from, each of which has certain advantages and drawbacks.

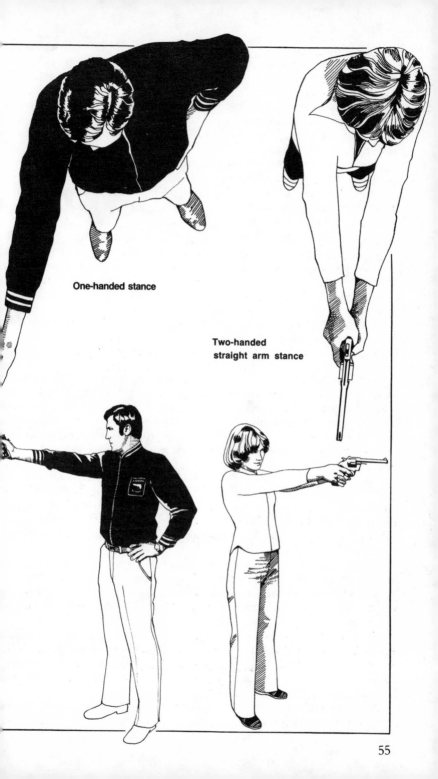

One-handed stance

Two-handed
straight arm stance

The easiest of the two stances to adopt is one which is taught in many American police departments. The simplicity of this position is probably its greatest asset, making it easy to learn and ideal for teaching personnel who have to carry sidearms in such organizations such as police, especially if available training time is limited. The stance is also well suited for shooting under circumstances when the sights cannot be used e.g. at night. On the debit side, the position tends to put some strain on the shoulder muscles making it uncomfortable to hold for any length of time.

In this position your feet are squared 90 degrees to the line of fire with the heels apart as in one-handed shooting.

Hold your body erect, grip the pistol, pushing both arms straight out in front of you, locking the elbows. You may hold your head erect or bent forward slightly to align the sights with the target.

The other two-handed shooting position is favoured in the sport of practical pistol shooting and is known as the 'Weaver' stance. It is quite complicated to learn but, once mastered, provides a very steady and firm position from which to shoot that is particularly suited for shooting at longer distances. It also gives good control over the recoil of the pistol when a number of shots are fired rapidly.

To assume this stance, stand as you would when shooting a rifle with your feet and shoulders angled roughly between 30 and 45 degrees to the line of fire. The distance between your heels is the same as in the positions just described.

Bend the arm of the supporting hand at the elbow as you would when holding a rifle. Now push the hand gripping the pistol out straight, at the same time gripping it with the supporting hand. The shooting hand should be as straight as possible although a slight flexing at the elbow is permissible. Try to think of the shooting arm as the stock of a rifle and remember that the further away the pistol is from your eyes, the better it is for accuracy.

As with shooting a rifle, you may have to drop your head slightly to the side of the shooting arm in order to align the sights with the target. A common mistake made by novices when learning the Weaver stance is to fail to keep the shoulders in line with the position of the feet. It helps if you consciously drop the shoulder of the supporting arm which will ensure that the bent elbow position is achieved.

Target shooters keep their legs straight but stand relaxed and do not lock the knees as this causes undue strain on the leg muscles. Some shooters, when using either of the two-handed shooting positions, have their knees slightly flexed to enable them to turn quickly if more than one target has to be engaged.

Perhaps the most common fault in the stance of many beginners, irrespective of which stance is being used, is failure to distribute the body weight evenly on both feet. After the stance has been assumed constantly check that you are not favouring one foot over the other i.e. by placing most of your weight on it.

A good pistol stance may be likened to a gun platform, which, as any artillery man will tell you, is essential for accuracy.

The Weaver stance

57

Aiming

As mentioned at the beginning of this chapter, correct aiming of a handgun is vital if accuracy is to be achieved. Because they have short barrels, just a slight error in aligning the sights with the target is greatly magnified, resulting in a poor shot on the target.

It is necessary for you to establish which is your master eye because this is the one you should use to aim the pistol. The dominance of one eye over the other occurs in everyone, even though both may possess identical sharpness of vision. To establish which of your eyes is dominant, simply hold out your hand in front of you, making a circle with the thumb and forefinger. Look through the circle at an object some distance away with both eyes and, alternately, close one eye and then the other. You will notice that the object looked at leaves the ring when the one eye is closed. Your master (dominant) eye is the one that sees the object remain in the ring when the other eye is closed.

Most people close one eye when aiming a gun because, if both eyes are used, a double image of the sights is seen which can be very distracting. In spite of this it is better to keep both eyes open when aiming as the closing of one eye puts a strain on the other and also tenses the facial muscles. The majority of the top shooters keep both eyes open when aiming and this can be achieved in a number of ways.

One can simply keep both eyes open, learning to ignore the distraction caused by the double image which, in time, will become barely noticeable. Alternatively, close the other eye slightly until only one image is seen. Another method is to close the other eye while taking aim, opening it after the sights have been aligned with the target. Many target shooters overcome the problem by wearing shooting spectacles with the lens covering the non-shooting eye masked. The same effect can be achieved by fitting a sheet of card to one's cap so that it hangs over the eye not used in aiming.

The actual aiming of the pistol consists of lining up the front and rear sights with the object that it is intended to shoot. The first step is to learn to align the front and rear sights correctly.

Pick up an unloaded handgun and point it at a plain background such as a wall. Place the frontsight blade in the center of the notch in the rear sight. Make sure that the top of the front sight is in line with the top of the rear. It is *imperative* that the front sight is *perfectly centered* in the rear sight notch because, any error, laterally or horizontally, will mean that the strike of your shot will not be in the centre of the target. You must also ensure that you keep the sights horizontal as, if they are canted over to one side, your shots will be to the left or right of the point of aim.

The eye has to look at the rear sight, front sight and target during aiming and it cannot keep all three objects in focus at the same time. Because perfect sight alignment is so essential for accuracy, the eye must be focused ON THE FRONT SIGHT. If this is done, the image of the target will appear blurred or fuzzy.

As shown in the following illustration, target shooters usually place their sights in the area of the bottom of the black centre of the target. This silhouettes the sights against the white background making it easier to

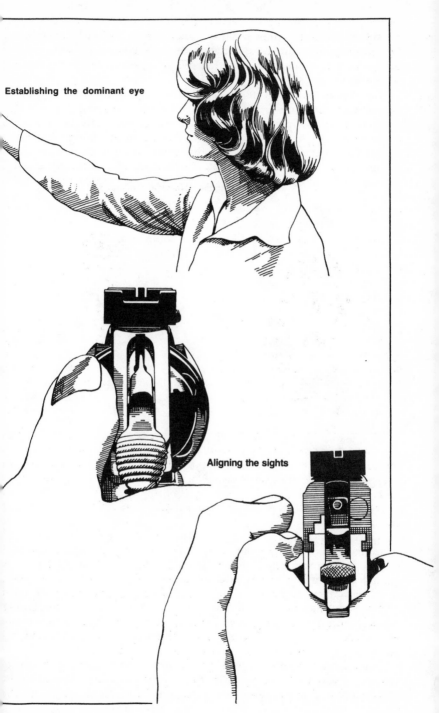

Establishing the dominant eye

Aligning the sights

59

ensure perfect alignment. If the point of aim was in the centre of the target, the sights would tend to be less discernable against the black background. Of course the sights are so adjusted that the shots will strike the centre of the black. Aiming in target shooting is covered in greater detail in Chapter 9 'Pistol Shooting as a Sport'.

In defense and practical shooting the same principles of aiming apply even though the figure targets used do not have any central aiming point. Concentrate on aligning the front and rear sights and aim for the area of the centre of the target. Don't worry about the lack of an aiming mark as the eyes will automatically centre the sights in the middle area of the target.

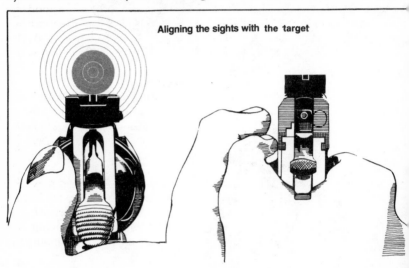

Aligning the sights with the target

In both defense and target shooting it is always better to aim at an area of the target rather than at one small point. If an aiming point is used there is a tendency to concentrate one's vision on the point rather than on the sights with the resultant loss of accuracy. By choosing an area to aim at you can concentrate on the sights and not worry if they stray off the centre of your area of aim.

Once the principles of aiming have been mastered you can turn to establishing your natural point of aim. This is standing in such a manner that, when the shooting arm is raised, it points directly at the target. A natural point of aim means that no undue strain is placed on the arm, shoulder and legs and is an aid to accurate shooting. Even in two-handed defense shooting where circumstances would never permit the establishing of one's natural point of aim prior to firing a shot, there is no harm in doing so in practice. After a while you will find that you automatically stand in a position that is close to if not actually your natural point of aim.

Your natural point of aim is established by first gripping the pistol correctly. Next, take up the correct stance in relation to the target. Hold the pistol so that it points down about 45 degrees to the ground with the shooting arm locked straight and look down to line up the sights correctly. Now look at the target, close your eyes and then raise the pistol into the shooting position. Open your eyes and see where the pistol is aimed. If it is to the left or right of the target move one of the feet slightly to bring the pistol on to the target. Do this until, when the pistol is raised, it points directly at the target.

By far the most common error that shooters make in aiming is *failure to focus their vision on the front sight*. Too often they are more worried about the relation of the sights with the point of aim on the target and consequently they look through the sights rather than at them. Remember that, provided the front sight is perfectly aligned with the rear you will still score a good hit even if your aim is slightly off centre. Every time you aim concentrate on sights, not target. SHARP SIGHTS AND FUZZY TARGET ADD UP TO AN ACCURATE SHOT BEING FIRED.

Trigger Control

Applying pressure to the trigger to release the firing mechanism is the final act of firing the pistol and, as with aiming, is critical if accuracy is to be achieved. Lack of proper trigger control will disturb your sight alignment resulting in a miss or a poor shot on the target. The trigger squeeze or pull must, therefore, be carefully controlled so that *the sights are not disturbed in any way*.

Single action fire is the easiest because only a relatively light pressure on the trigger is needed to dischage the pistol. Start by gripping the handgun correctly, cocking the action with the other hand. If you are using a revolver don't cock the hammer with the thumb of the hand holding the handgun because this will alter your grip; use the thumb of the supporting hand.

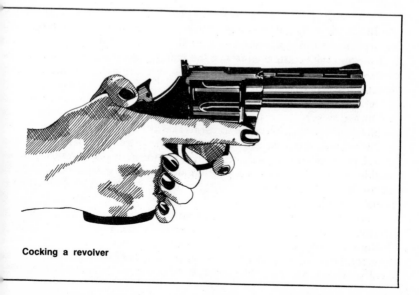

Cocking a revolver

When the handgun has been cocked, lightly engage the trigger with the index finger and, when the pistol has been brought on to the target and the sights aligned, gradually increase your pressure on the trigger. Continue to concentrate on aligning the sights as you squeeze the trigger until, before you realise it, the pistol has fired. As the muzzle rises from the recoil, follow through by continuing to concentrate on the sights. Don't forget that the direction of your pull on the trigger is directly to the rear. Think of pulling towards your aiming eye.

Don't worry too much if the sights move about the target a little as you squeeze the trigger. Everyone shakes while holding a pistol although the shake is less noticeable with an experienced shooter than with a novice. Much of the shaking or wavering can be reduced by correct breathing.

The United States Marksmanship Training Unit maintain that a shooter is at his steadiest when his breath is exhaled. To shoot using this method, take three normal breaths exhaling as you raise the pistol on to the target and holding your breath as you aim and squeeze the trigger. Some shooters prefer to shoot holding on a partially exhaled breath but, whichever method you decide to use, don't remain in the aim too long. If your waver develops into a shake then lower the pistol and rest as this is a sure sign of being too long in the aim.

Double action shooting is more difficult because of the long, stiff trigger pull. Nevertheless, it can be mastered quite easily if approached in the right way. You should start learning to shoot double action before going on to single action if you have bought such a handgun for defense purposes.

There are two methods of double action trigger control and much depends upon the handgun you are using. In the single-stage method the trigger is pulled through evenly without any hesitation until the hammer falls and is suitable for handguns that have a smooth double action trigger pull.

Where the trigger action seems to have a hitch or gets harder then use the two-stage pull. Here the trigger is pulled back until the hitch or hardness is felt. At this point it is held momentarily while any sight correction is made and then completed to fire the handgun. It may sound like a slow method of shooting but, in fact, very fast shooting can be done in this manner, especially at the longer ranges.

Where more than one shot is to be fired the *release* of the trigger of a double action revolver is just as important as the pull. Many novice shooters let the trigger snap forward uncontrolled after firing a shot. This results in the sights being jerked off the target making re-alignment of the aim more difficult for the next shot. The trigger must always be released under control so that the sights remain roughly aligned for the next shot. The maxim is: CONTROLLED TRIGGER PULL AND CONTROLLED TRIGGER RELEASE.

If you are shooting a double action automatic your subsequent shots will be fired single action. The difficulty of getting used to the sudden change from double action to single action has been rather exaggerated by those who have never mastered this type of weapon. It is quite incorrect to say that the grip has to be changed after the first double action shot has been fired. The main problem is to overcome the tendency to snatch (jerk the trigger) when going on to single action fire. This can be overcome by shooting slowly to begin with and remembering to squeeze the single action shots once the double action pull has been completed. Speed will come with practice.

As with single action shooting you must concentrate on keeping the sights aligned as you pull the trigger. Obviously, because of the long, stiff double action pull, the tendency for your sights to waver about the target will be greater than in single action shooting. This will decrease the more you practise and the muscles in your hand, arm and shoulder get stronger. Begin slowly and increase your speed only when you can keep your shots grouped in the centre of the target.

So much has recently been made of the difficulty of mastering double action revolver shooting by those who favour automatics that many people have been put off. While it is true that double action is more difficult to learn, effective, fast defensive shooting is possible in a relatively short time, once the muscles in the hand, arm and shoulder have been developed and strengthened.

It is well worth recounting the exploits of Ed McGivern of Montana, USA who, between the wars, developed double action revolver shooting to a fine art. Among his many feats was the ability to hit multiple targets thrown into the air including the placing of six shots in a small tin before it hit the ground. His speed shooting with a double action revolver was almost unbelievable. In 1919 on November 30, at Denver, Colorado, using a Colt double action 38, he set a world speed record by firing six shots in 3/5ths (0,6) of a second. This feat was repeated the following year with the same revolver. On January 23rd, 1934, using a Smith & Wesson 38 revolver he established another world record by shooting five shots in 2/5ths (0,4) of a second. The range of both feats was five yards and the group of shots in each instance, could be covered by a playing card. Neither of these records has ever been broken and what is even more remarkable is the fact that McGivern shot all his records using a one-handed hold. It is also interesting to note that he first used Colt 45 Automatics in his speed attempts but switched to double action revolvers because he found them better suited for speed shooting.

Ed McGivern was, of course, an exceptional shooter, without doubt one of the greatest revolver shots the world has ever seen. Nevertheless his feats prove that double action revolver shooting is very effective for defensive shooting and should not be lightly dismissed.

Shooting With the Weak Hand

The use of the weak hand (the one not normally used to grip the handgun) to fire a pistol is confined to defensive shooting. Normally, one would make use of every possible advantage, such as using two hands to grip the pistol which permits very fast and effective shooting. Nevertheless, flexibility is very important including the ability to shoot with either hand. The two handed hold cannot always be used especially if one hand is incapacitated.

Shooting with the strong hand (the one normally used to grip the handgun) unsupported is difficult enough so it is natural to presume that using the weak one will be even harder. This is true, mainly because the weak hand is used so little in every day life; but, as always, with a little practice, good shooting can still be achieved.

First get used to gripping the pistol correctly then assume the stance which will be the exact reverse of that used in normal one-handed shooting. Aiming and trigger control are the same.

At first, everything will feel very strange and difficulty will be experienced in holding the handgun steady when aiming and pulling the trigger. With perseverance, the shaking will disappear and you will soon be achieving good results with your weak hand.

In conclusion, the methods of gripping and standing when shooting a pistol that have been described are those used by the majority of top shooters. There are those whose grip and stance fall considerably short of what the purist considers the ideal, yet they still get excellent results. It is results, not shooting style, that count in the end so variations on the methods described are quite acceptable if the individual finds that they suit his particular needs. Only the two main principles of pistol shooting, aiming and firing the pistol remain constant for everyone so we come back to what we said in the beginning of this Chapter — ACCURATE PISTOL SHOOTING DEPENDS UPON AIMING THE WEAPON CORRECTLY AT THE TARGET AND FIRING IT WITHOUT DISTURBING THE ALIGNMENT OF THE SIGHTS.

Chapter Seven

LEARNING TO SHOOT

There are three progressive stages in learning to shoot a handgun. First and foremost, a considerable amount of pre-range preparation is necessary to master the principles of firearms safety and shooting a pistol before the novice will be ready to fire with live ammunition. This is done at home by practising loading, unloading, making safe, learning the basic shooting principles and field stripping for cleaning with an unloaded pistol, using the technique known as 'dry shooting' or 'dry firing'. Once the shooter is ready for the range learning how to shoot accurately is the priority and, only when this has been achieved, should the ability to shoot quickly begin.

Dry Shooting Practise

'Dry shooting' or 'dry firing' consists of going through all the motions of shooting a firearm using an unloaded gun. It is an excellent way to learn how to use your pistol but it should not stop there. Apart from its obvious value of teaching you how to shoot, it also helps strengthen all the muscles used to fire a pistol and is, therefore, an excellent training aid. This, together with the fact that it costs nothing, requires no special equipment and can be done in the home, probably accounts for the fact that most of the top shooters include plenty of dry shooting in their training programmes. Not only can it be used to learn the basics of pistol shooting but also for advanced techniques such as drawing from the holster and speed re-loading which are dealt with further on in this book.

There are varying opinions on the damage a handgun is likely to incur through repeated dry firing. A small amount will probably have no adverse effect but extensive dry shooting may damage the hammer or firing pin. Although this is debatable, some modern target pistols make provision for dry firing. If you are worried about possibly damaging your handgun, there are several things that you can do about it.

The best method is to load your gun with 'Snap Cartridges' which are made especially for dry shooting, cushioning the blow of the hammer on the firing pin. Unfortunately, these are difficult to obtain so you will probably have to turn to the alternative method, which is to use fired cartridge cases. Although the primers have already been struck, they will still cushion the blow of the hammer a few times. Obviously, to be effective, they must be frequently replaced.

It is very important, from the safety angle, to make *perfectly sure that the gun is unloaded,* and, if empty cartridges cases are being used, that *live ones* have not been inadvertently loaded. Quite apart from the danger of accidently discharging a shot indoors, chunks of plaster blasted out of the living room wall take a lot of explaining to landlords and the police, not to mention wives or husbands.

Before you start to put everything together, experiment with the various grips and stances that were covered in the preceding chapter to decide which suit your needs best. Once this has been established you will be ready to start learning how to fire an accurate shot. In dry shooting you duplicate everything that will be done when actually shooting with live ammunition In describing how to grip, stand, aim and pull the trigger the sequence that each stage occurs in firing a shot has been deliberately followed. You must get into the habit of following this sequence every time you fire a deliberately aimed shot.

Check first that the handgun is not loaded with live ammunition. Take up the correct grip, then assume the stance you are going to use and check your natural point of aim. Now prepare to fire the shot by taking a few breaths and, when ready, exhale, raising the pistol on to the target. When in the aim concentrate on aligning the sights as you carefully squeeze the trigger to fire the shot.

In dry fire shooting your follow through should tell you if the sights were disturbed when you fired the pistol. Any signs of the sights being jerked out of alignment as the hammer falls are a sure indication that your trigger control was not perfect. This is going to happen in the beginning but will quickly disappear with practise. When the shot has been fired, lower the pistol and rest before trying again.

As your aiming and trigger control improves try to 'call' your shots. This is committing yourself to predicting where the bullet has struck, or, in the case of dry shooting, would have struck the target after the shot has been fired. By watching your sights for any signs of jerking just as the gun fires you will be able to judge if it was a good shot or not. Many experienced target shooters can say almost exactly where their shots are on the target.

It is a good idea to check your grip and stance before you lower the gun after firing a shot. In the early stages of your practise you may find errors in your grip and stance after the shot has been fired. Provided you are aware of them you will be able to take the necessary corrective action.

Target shooters will confine themselves to learning to shoot using only one hand but, while the two-handed method is favoured for defense shooting, it is a good idea to begin dry firing using one hand as well. There are two very good reasons for this. First, you want to build up the muscle in your shooting hand, arm and shoulder to perfect trigger control and this is the best way of doing it. Second, by tackling the hardest method first, when you turn to using two hands you will find it so much easier. Conversely, if you start by practising with two hands, when you try one-handed shooting, you will find it doubly difficult to master.

Don't overdo dry shooting in the early stages so that you become tired and start to develop faults. Start modestly by firing ten to 15 dry shots and build up until you can manage 30 to 40. Regular dry shooting for about a week before going to the range will pay dividends to your performance.

Firing Live Ammunition

It is important that you hit what you are aiming at when you start using live ammunition. Strikes on the target, even if they are not good, will at least give you some indication of what you are doing wrong. For this reason you are advised to begin very close to the target which should, at first, consist simply of a plain sheet of paper or card about 2 ft. X 3 ft. in size. Using a target without an aiming mark will help you concentrate on the sights and get used to area aiming.

Firing the First Shot

The firing of a handgun can be a traumatic experience if you have never shot before. Like most novices, you don't know what to expect and will be wondering if the gun will kick much or how loud the report will be. No matter what assurances you have been given, your apprehension will disappear only after you have fired your first shot.

Begin by firing just one shot. Position yourself three yards from the target and load with only one round. No doubt your heart will be beating a little fast so just stop for a minute and think about what you are going to do. Go through the sequence of grip, stance and establishing your natural point of aim, preparing yourself for the shot. When ready, go through the remaining procedure of firing the shot. When in the aim try to overcome your excitement and concentrate on sights and trigger control. After the shot has been fired you will find, much to your surprise that the experience was not nearly so bad as you thought it would be. Better still, when you check the target you will find that your hit is very close to your area of aim.

Developing Accuracy

The first step towards accuracy is learning to shoot tight groups. Grouping is the ability to place a number of shots very close together on the target when using the same point of aim. The tighter (smaller in size) the group, the better you are aligning the sights and controlling the trigger.

Load up with three, or better still five rounds and, using the same type of target at the same distance (three yards), fire each shot carefully. Take your time, think what you are doing and use the same procedure you have been using in dry shooting practice, concentrating on aiming at the same area on the target each time you shoot. If everything has been going according to plan your shots should be grouped in a small pattern on the target. The odd shot outside the group can be ignored as a bad one particularly if you were able to call it. Don't worry unduly if your group is not exactly where you were aiming. It may be that your sights need adjusting although you might find that, as you progress, the group moves closer to your area of aim. If you are satisfied with your performance, patch or replace the target, and move back to five yards and repeat the exercise. Gradually increase your distance from the target in three or four yard stages until you can shoot a reasonable group at 15 yards.

As your distance from the target increases you will find that your group increases in size. This is quite normal because aiming and trigger control become more critical the further away from the target you are. In defense shooting, once you can consistently group all your shots within a diameter of about 10 ins, you are ready to progress to the next stage which will be repeating the same practise but using first the strong and then the weak hand un-supported. Here you need only work back in stages to about 10 yards. With target shooting, because the pistol will have superior sights and trigger action, you should only move on to the next stage when you have reduced the size of your group to about 4 inches. The various target matches and how to shoot them are described in detail in Chapter 9.

Sometimes things go wrong in spite of all your previous dry shooting preparation. You will soon become aware if things are not going according to plan if your shots are scattered all over the target with, perhaps, a few complete misses. In all probability you are snatching which means that you are anticipating just when the shot is about to fire and are jerking the trigger. This is a very commmon fault in both single and double action shooting, especially if the handgun has a hard trigger or one that has a lot of creep (play or drag before the hammer is released).

The best way to establish if you are snatching and to overcome it is to get another shooter to load your handgun for you before each shot. He hands it over to you either empty or loaded so that you never know, until you have pulled the trigger what its condition is. You will soon know if you are snatching because you will see the sights jerk as you fire the gun when it is empty. The cure is to continue shooting, not knowing when the gun will fire, until the tendency to snatch has been overcome.

Developing Speed

The ability to shoot quickly is necessary in both defensive and target shooting. Although the principles are the same, shooting quickly in those target events that have to be fired in a limited amount of time are fully covered in chapter 9.

First, you must learn how to bring the pistol quickly into the aim to fire the first shot. You should start with the pistol held in the ready position, progressing later to drawing from the holster. A good 'ready position' is similar to that used in target shooting, where the shooter faces the target holding the pistol so that it points to the ground at an angle of 45 degrees. It is assumed by first taking the correct grip, stance and establishing your natural point of aim. Once this has been done, come into the aim, line up the sights with the target, then slowly lower the pistol to 45 degrees keeping your eyes on the sights to ensure that they remain correctly aligned. If you

Coming into the aim from the ready position

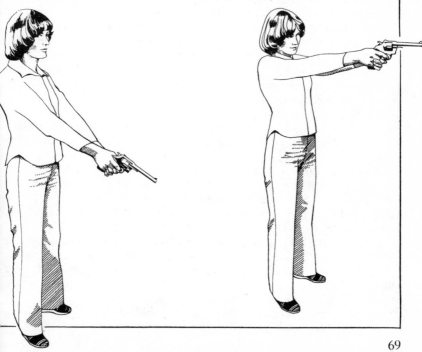

are using a two-handed hold, keep both hands on the pistol as you lower it.

It helps in picking up the sights more quickly when the pistol comes on to the target if you deliberately lift the muzzle of the pistol when in the ready position so that the front sight protrudes above the rear.

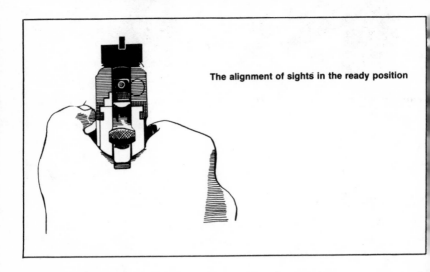

The alignment of sights in the ready position

If you are using a double action revolver or automatic, lightly engage the trigger with the index finger. When you are ready, look at the target and raise the pistol up in a smooth sweeping motion. As the sights come into view, concentrate on any adjustments to sight alignment and fire the shot. Don't hurry but strive for a smoothness of action rather than speed. As you improve you can speed up the action by commencing your double action pull while raising the pistol on to the target so that when the sights are aligned, the gun is almost ready to fire.

With a single action automatic, do not touch the trigger but apply the safety. As you bring the gun up, wipe off the safety before it comes on to the target. The time to place your index finger on the trigger is when the sights come into view.

It must be obvious that, should you have to use a pistol to defend yourself, you will never have time to prepare yourself by establishing your natural point of aim. The reason for doing this in the initial stages of training is to get you used to shooting in your natural stance so that, in time, you automatically assume it without preparation.

Once you can bring your pistol on to the target reasonably quickly you will be ready for the next stage which is the firing of a series of quick shots. Here, the main problem is controlling the recoil so that you can recover quickly for the next shot. An important essential is a good firm grip on the pistol to help reduce recoil. Many shooters find that the tendency of automatics to twist when recoiling can be controlled by gripping with the thumb placed high as described in the previous chapter.

The final stage in speed shooting is being able to engage several different targets. To do this quickly, without overshooting the target on to which you are swinging, lock the upper part of your body from the waist up. By doing this you swing with the hips and knees, not the arm. Of course, when either of the two-handed methods are used, the upper body is automatically locked.

Just how fast you must shoot depends on a number of factors. Probably most important is how far away the target is because speed is relative to distance. In learning to shoot accurately you will have realized that the closer the target is the easier it is to hit. Consequently, you must shoot very quickly when close to the target, not only because it is easier for you, but because it will also be easy for your attacker. An aimed shot up to about seven yards does not require perfect sight alignment or trigger control to hit the target. All you need is a flash image of the sights to verify that they are roughly aligned before quickly squeezing the trigger. Beyond seven yards you will have to spend more time on aiming and trigger control the further away from the target you move.

You must also shoot only as fast as you can effectively hit the target. Being the first to fire the shot does not end the fight; only an effective hit will do that. Training for speed, as with accuracy, consists of plenty of dry shooting, starting close to the target, moving back only when you are satisfied with your results at that range and concentrating on smoothness of action rather that speed in the initial stages. Follow this procedure and your ability to shoot quickly and effectively will follow very quickly.

Chapter Eight

DEFENSIVE PISTOL SHOOTING

Three attributes make a handgun an ideal personal defense weapon even though it is the most difficult type of firearm to shoot. It is compact, easy to carry and can be brought into action very quickly and effectively at close range. It has been found that most of the situations involving pistols as defense weapons take place at very short distances, usually at night. Of course, there is no guarantee at what range one might have to defend oneself with a handgun but, although pistols can shoot accurately over quite long distances, they are designed as close range weapons.

In learning defensive pistol shooting techniques, training must be realistic and closely related to the type of situation you might encounter. As the nature of the potential threat to individuals will often be different, some people will require more skill with a handgun than others. People such as the police, who have to carry a handgun as part of their everyday work, need an extremely high degree of proficiency in all aspects of defensive pistol shooting. They must be able to shoot at both short and long ranges, at any time of the day or night, from a variety of different positions. They must also have the ability to draw from a holster and reload quickly. At the bottom of the scale, those who simply want a pistol for home defense will probably only have to learn how to shoot effectively up to a maximum distance of 10 yards, possibly at night, as their shooting will probably be inside their residences. Each reader will have to select from the techniques described in this chapter just what he, or she, needs to learn to repel the type of attack anticipated.

Drawing From the Holster

A substantial holster of good design is necessary if you intend carrying your handgun on your person unless you have selected a lightweight pocket weapon. With the wide range of holsters available you should have little trouble in finding one to suit your needs. Like the majority of other gun owners, you may want to carry your gun concealed and this presents few problems unless you possess a very large pistol. Only women will have problems because the female form does not lend itself easily to hiding a handgun. Fortunately, few women have a need to carry a pistol, so the problem does not arise very often. Where there is a need to go armed, women must either restrict themselves to wearing clothing that will conceal the weapon or select a robust handbag with a strong shoulder strap in which to carry it. If possible, the bag should have a special compartment to hold the pistol in such a way that it is secure yet reasonably accessible. This modification should be possible to persons skilled in leather work. Armed uniformed personnel, on the other hand, are often issued with a standard holster that does not hide the handgun.

In spite of the erroneous impression given by Western films, the most important feature of a holster is not to provide a super-fast draw. There are holsters designed for quick-draw but these are limited to sporting use. When choosing a holster for your gun, look for one that is comfortable to wear, protects and keeps the gun secure, permitting it to be brought into action reasonably quickly. Many of the holsters available will have models made for the gun you possess. Some sacrifice in the speed in which the gun can be drawn must be expected if the holster is required to retain the weapon very securely, or to protect it from the elements.

Although a wide variety of holsters is available those in general use fall into three types. These are the hip draw, cross draw and shoulder holster. The shoulder holster's greatest value is in concealing very large handguns or the carrying of scope-sighted pistols for hunting purposes. Contrary to popular belief, the shoulder holster does not conceal an average-sized handgun any better than the other two and is very uncomfortable to wear. For this reason it will not be dealt with in this chapter.

There are three popular versions of the hip holster. The high-ride hip holster carries the pistol high with the butt tipped forward above the top of the belt. The holster is usually situated just behind the trouser seam and allows the gun to be carried exposed or concealed provided that, in the latter instance, the barrel length is not too long.

The belt Loop holster is a very simple design, consisting of a loop of leather that is fitted to the belt and carries the pistol in the same position as the high-ride type. It is comfortable, permits the gun to be carried concealed yet is reasonably fast. It is especially suited for automatics and has an additional advantage that, if one's jacket is removed and the gun taken out of the holster, the belt loop does not advertise the fact that the wearer is armed.

The Border Patrol duty holster is intended to carry the handgun exposed to view on a Sam Browne belt. It is popular with many police departments in the United States of America and is comfortable, smart when worn with a uniform, carries the gun securely and permits it to be drawn very quickly. The butt of the handgun is tipped forward but is lower, being level with the top of the belt, which allows the gun to be drawn very rapidly from the holster. When carrying an automatic or a

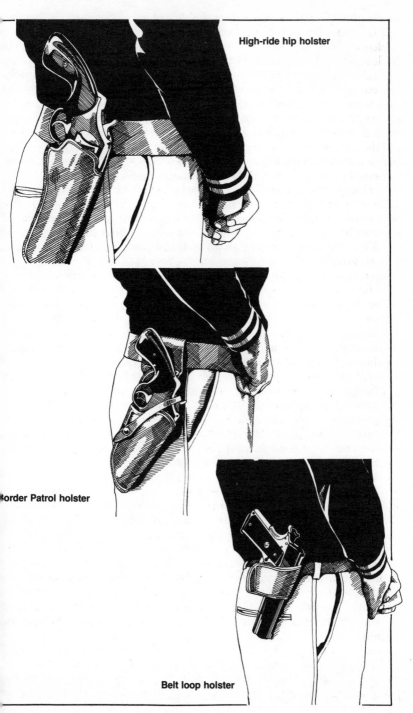

High-ride hip holster

Border Patrol holster

Belt loop holster

four-inch (100 mm) barrel revolver the wearer can sit comfortably in a car. Swivel versions permit larger revolvers to be carried if the wearer has to travel in a vehicle, and a retaining strap or thumbsnap for securing the handgun can also be obtained.

The cross draw holster carries the handgun on the shooter's hip on the opposite side to his shooting hand. The angle of the holster tips the butt of the gun to the rear and it is worn well forward of the trouser seam. It permits the gun to be carried exposed on a uniform Sam Browne belt or concealed. Although quite popular, it does not conceal the weapon as well nor is it as comfortable to wear as a hip holster. It also has the disadvantage in that the gun has to be drawn and swung across on to the target. This can result in overswinging to the extent that the target is missed.

The flap holster does not permit a fast draw but carries the weapon very securely and protects it against rain and dust. It is most suitable for carrying the gun in the bush when hunting or working where you are exposed to all types of weather conditions. For this reason it is often chosen for use by uniformed personnel. Although it is not designed for a fast draw, if it is worn in the cross-draw position and has an easy to release catch securing the flap, the gun can be brought into action surprisingly quickly.

There are a number of variations of the holsters just described. Some high-ride hip designs are fitted with a very efficient method of securing the pistol until needed. These have a thumbbreak strap that fits over the hammer preventing the gun from being removed unless it is released by the thumb of the shooting hand. Holsters worn inside the waist band in either the hip or cross draw position conceal the gun very effectively but make it more difficult to bring the gun into action. A very good design is the Berns-Martin which is open at the front, allowing the pistol to be pushed through and on to the target. A strong spring keeps the holster closed and the gun secure. Stay away from the clamshell holster which provides a very fast draw by opening out like a shell when a button near the trigger guard is pressed. The release mechanism can jam, preventing the gun from being drawn, or accidentally open if the button is inadvertently touched. They are banned from being used by many police departments.

When choosing a holster for an automatic that will be carried cocked and locked, make quite sure that the safety cannot be accidentally released. This can occur in a badly fitted holster which allows the pistol to move in it. It is also advisable to check very closely the fitting with the holster of those automatics equipped with the button type of magazine release catch. For the same reasons, friction can depress the catch and release the magazine.

Just as important as the holster you choose is the belt you wear with it. The best belts are made from strong cow-hide that match the holster loop. They should be fairly wide, between 2 inches and 2½ inches, and fit around the waist tight enough to prevent the holster from moving its position or sagging.

Once you have chosen the holster you will want to learn how to use it. Although you may be itching to start practising, resist the temptation until you have mastered all the basic principles of shooting described in the previous two chapters. *It cannot be too strongly emphasized that drawing from*

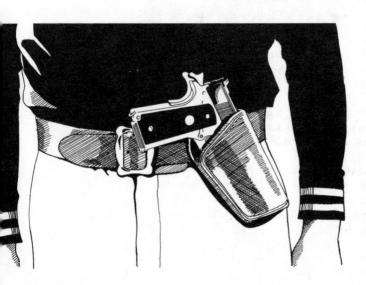

A cross-draw holster

A flap holster

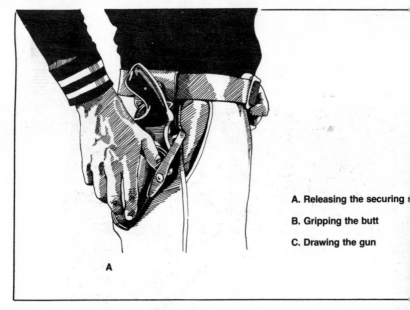

A. Releasing the securing [strap]

B. Gripping the butt

C. Drawing the gun

A

the holster with a loaded pistol is extremely dangerous if attempted by a novice
When you do start, prevent any chance of accidents by practising you
technique with plenty of dry shooting before you start with the pisto
loaded. Failure to do so could result in you accidentally shooting yourself in
the leg, hip or groin. *Do not indulge in irresponsible horseplay by challenging*
another shooter to a fast draw match with unloaded pistols. Such behaviour has al
too often ended in tragedy.

Drawing the handgun from your holster involves first gripping i
correctly and then bringing it on to the target as quickly as possible. When
done properly, these two actions become one complete fluid motion.

The simplest, safest handgun to draw from a holster is either a doubl
action revolver or automatic. If you are using any of the hip holsters, which
seem to be the most popular, the draw is begun by moving your hand to the
butt of the gun in a sweeping motion that brings it up under the grip rathe
than straight back on to it. If your holster has a securing strap or thumb
break catch, release this with the thumb as your hand moves up to grip the
butt.

Obviously, if your holster has no securing device, then your hand wil
move straight up to the handgun. As your hand makes contact with the gun
butt, curl your fingers around it and slip the thumb into the proper position,
keeping the index finger away from the trigger.

Once the gun has been gripped, your hand continues on its upward
travel, drawing the gun from the holster.

As the barrel clears the top of the holster, the handgun is pushed forward on
to the target and the trigger is engaged by the index finger. The shooting
position that you adopt once the gun has been drawn depends very much
upon how far away your target is. Wherever possible you should try to fire

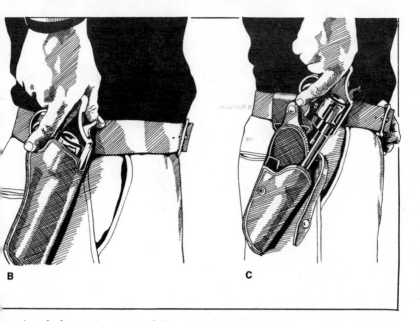

B   **C**

an aimed shot using one of the two–handed shooting positions already described. Taking up the Weaver stance is covered in the description of the single action automatic draw but, if the straight arm method is to be used, bring your supporting hand across to grip the shooting hand as your gun comes on to the target.

A large number of American Police departments teach their personnel to assume a crouch position when firing. The idea behind this is to present an adversary with a smaller target although its validity is debatable. Many argue that the time wasted in assuming the crouch does not justify it and one is better off striving for a quick effective shot from the normal upright position. While there is merit in this point of view, it is also true that, if shot at, the natural tendency is to duck, which is a strong argument in favour of the crouch position. In passing, it must be mentioned that the crouch favours the straight arm two–handed shooting position and is not really suitable for the Weaver stance.

Assuming a crouch when using the two–handed position is quite simple. As you bring the pistol up on to the target, start to sink at the knees and drop into a slight semi–seated position.

If, for some reason, only one hand can be used, the crouch position known as the 'shoulder point' position is very effective. Here you sink into the slight seated position after the gun has been drawn from the holster and then point the weapon at the target using the arm and shoulder.

Somewhat more complicated is bringing a single action automatic into action from the holster. Depending upon the type of automatic, there are two methods of carrying these handguns, the safest being to load with a full magazine, keeping the chamber empty. This method has the disadvantage that it takes longer to draw and shoot, but for some automatics, it is the only

Two-handed crouch position

Shoulder point position

safe carrying method. Automatics with suitable safety catches may be carried cocked and locked which provides for a much faster draw but is *more hazardous, requiring a considerable amount of training.*

The technique of drawing an automatic from a hip holster is the same as previously described except that *great care must be taken when gripping the pistol to ensure that the thumb does not wipe off the safety in the holster.* If a cross draw holster is used, the draw is begun by moving your hand across the front of your body to grip the gun from the rear. Where a flap holster is used, the free hand unfastens the flap and pulls it up, exposing the butt of the pistol.

As your hand makes contact with the butt of the pistol your fingers wrap around it. It is very important to make sure that your thumb is placed in a position above the safety, ready to wipe it off, while the *index finger is laid outside the holster so that the trigger is not in any way touched.* The placing of the thumb is very important and great care must be exercised to ensure that the safety is not disengaged while still in the holster.

After the grip has been taken, draw the pistol out of the holster and, when clear, start to turn it towards the target. When the gun is pointing towards the target, bring the other hand across to support the one gripping the pistol if the Weaver stance is being used. If the weapon is cocked and locked, then the safety is disengaged as the other hand starts to grip the one holding the pistol. Where the other method of carry is used then your free hand must first grip the slide and chamber a round before it supports the other one.

As you move the pistol up on to the target your index finger can lightly engage the trigger as the gun comes on to the target.

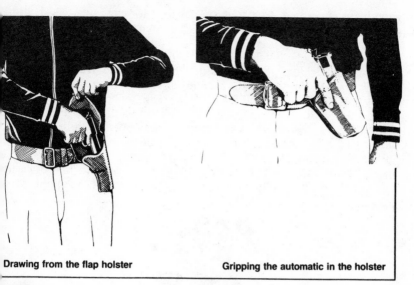

Drawing from the flap holster

Gripping the automatic in the holster

Releasing the safety catch

In the aim

Once on the target, align the sights and apply pressure to fire the pistol. At the beginning of this chapter it was stated that, as far as defensive shooting is concerned, handguns are designed for close quarters shooting and there is a lot of evidence to support this contention. In a number of surveys into shootings between police and criminals it has been confirmed that the majority of gunfights occurred at distances of seven yards or closer. Research into famous gunfights of the American Wild West, such as the 'Gunfight at OK Corral' and the shooting of William Bonney Alias Billy the Kid by Sheriff Pat Garrett indicates that the range, in both cases, was a matter of a few yards. Gunfights have taken place at longer ranges, a case in point being the shooting of Dave Tutt by James Butler (Wild Bill) Hickok, once Marshall of Abilene, which was at a range of about 70 yards in Springfield on July 21, 1865, but these are exceptions.

Where an attack is at close range under seven yards there is often no time to bring the pistol into the aim and you have to resort to shooting soon

Hip shooting at point blank range

Hip shooting from crouch position

Hip shooting between 2-5 metres

ter the gun has cleared the holster. In cases where your assailant is almost
top of you, shoot when your hand has just passed your belt.

Where your attacker is two or three yards away, push the pistol out in
ont of you, keeping the elbow into your side, concentrating your vision on
at part of your attacker's body you wish to hit. With practice very fast,
fective shooting can be done in this manner.

At ranges of seven yards and less the Federal Bureau of Investigation of
merica trains its agents to shoot from the hip in the crouch position. This
assumed by dropping into the semi-seated position as the gun clears the
lster which is then punched forward towards the target and fired. In
ng from the hip some shooters find the crouch of great assistance while
ers prefer to shoot from the normal upright position. The position that
est for you is a decision that only you can make.

The best method of concealing a handgun is to carry it in either a cross
w or high-ride hip holster worn under a jacket which must not be
ttoned at the front. The method of drawing the gun remains basically the
ne, the only difference being in how it is reached under the coat.

With a high-ride hip holster, there are three methods that can be used.
e simplest is to sweep the flap of the coat back with the hand which then
kes contact with the butt of the gun and draws it in the normal manner.
eep the coat back with some speed so that it continues back past the gun
d does not interfere with your gripping the pistol.

An alternative method is to sway the hips to the side opposite the holster
ich swings the coat away from the gun allowing your hand to reach for it
hout hindrance.

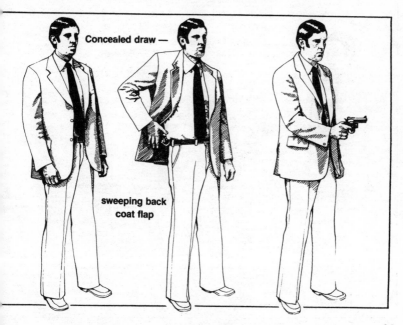

Concealed draw —

sweeping back
coat flap

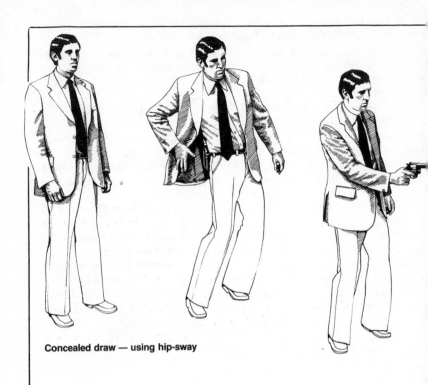

Concealed draw — using hip-sway

Concealed draw — using side step

The use of the side step is suited if you are going to assume the crouch position. Here you take a quick step to the side away from the holster bending forward slightly from the waist as you do so. This has a similar effect to the hip-sway: the coat flap is swung away from the pistol, allowing your hand to reach for it unimpeded.

There are two ways for getting into action from a concealed cross draw holster. You can simply slip your hand under the jacket and reach for the gun or lift the jacket flap out of the way with the free hand to expose the pistol.

Concealed cross draw — lifting coat

The same rules relating to how fast you should shoot apply equally when drawing from the holster i.e. speed is important when close to the target but the need decreases the further away you are.

In learning the draw, the object is to do it *without shooting yourself* in the process, which can happen if you are not careful. There will be no danger of this if you follow the sequence of training used in 'Learning to Shoot' (Chapter Seven). It will pay you handsomely if you spend some time experimenting to find the best position to wear your belt and holster before you start practising. Once you have established the best position, don't change it. The most difficult part of drawing from the holster is getting the right grip on the pistol and the sooner your hand learns where the holster and gun are, the better. If you will be carrying the gun concealed, begin your training without a coat until you have developed a reasonable degree of proficiency.

Begin by practising the draw with an empty gun, starting very slowly, working towards smoothness and economy of movement. Although each type of draw has been explained by breaking it down into its various stages, drawing and shooting is in fact one continuous, smooth action. Begin by slowly moving your hand to the butt of the pistol, gripping it correctly and drawing it out of the holster and up on to the target, aligning the sights and squeezing the trigger as the target comes into view. Concentrate on perfecting a smooth draw and speed will come with practice.

When you begin to shoot with live ammunition, start close to the target and move back as you gain confidence. *Slow down* to begin with, even though you may have built up fair amount of speed during dry shooting. *Don't rush your draw but always shoot only as fast as you are able to hit what you are aiming at.* If you hurry your draw, not only is there a good chance of missing, but a very real danger of accidentally shooting yourself, as nearly happened to Sheriff Pat Garrett when tracking down Billy the Kid. At Puerto de Luna he was accosted by the local town tough, one Mariano Leiva who, with his hand on his pistol, abused Garrett on the porch of a store. When he attempted to strike the Sheriff, a scuffle ensued. Garrett threw Leiva off the porch who then went for his gun and fired but missed. In retaliating, Garrett tried to draw his revolver too quickly, and the first shot went off prematurely, the bullet striking the ground between the two men. He made no mistake with his second shot, however, putting Leiva out of action with a shot in the shoulder. Not only does this incident clearly illustrate the danger of trying to hurry one's shooting; it shows that even good shots like Garrett can miss at close range. There is further evidence of this in accounts of a gunfight between Wild Bill Hickok and Phil Coe which took place at a range of only about eight feet. It is recorded that both men traded several shots before one from Hickok found its mark and ended the fight. The account is even more interesting when it is realised that, whatever else he may have been, Wild Bill Hicock has been acknowledged by all western historians as being an excellent pistol shot who never missed an opportunity to show off his marksmanship.

While it is comparatively easy for even a poor shot to hit a target at short distances, it becomes difficult when this must be done quickly. For this reason it is strongly recommended that you should spend a fair proportion of your time practising with and without a holster at close range, even as near as two metres. Here is where you really need to shoot quickly and effectively and, although some contend that there is always time to bring the pistol up to eye level, at the very short distances under seven yards you often do not have time for aiming.

Shooting from hip level is restricted to the ranges closest to the target up to a maximum range of about five yards. Although very fast and effective hip shooting can be done at seven years, beyond five or six yards there should be time to get the pistol up to eye level, even if the sights are not used. Hip shooting is, of course, an advanced technique and one that should only be attempted after a reasonble degree of proficiency in all aspects of aimed shooting has been attained.

The technique of shooting without the aid of the sights involves focusing your vision on the area of the target you want to hit and firing the gun when you think it is properly lined up. In pointing the handgun the hand and orearm are used, so keep the wrist locked. The further out in front you old the pistol, the better you will shoot. So if the target is over two yards way, get that gun out in front of you.

It is best to begin learning hip shooting with the gun in your hand before ou try it from the holster. When dry shooting, point the pistol at various bjects and fire when you think you are on the target; then freeze in that osition and ask someone to see where the pistol is aimed. Another method is slide a long wooden dowel down the barrel of the gun, wrapping tape round the portion in the bore to prevent it from falling out. Hold the pistol y your side and quickly point it at various objects using the dowel to tell ou if you are on target.

Up to about 15 yards it is possible to shoot instinctively by raising the veapon to just below eye level and looking at the target over the pistol's arrel. The need to do this in good light when the sights can be used is ebatable, but it is a good method of preparing oneself for shooting at ight.

When on the range use a big target so that you can have some idea of vhere your shots are going if they are not in the centre. It also helps if the ackstop into which your bullets will eventually land is composed of dry oil as the dust raised by the strikes of any shots that miss the target will give ou an indication of the extent of your error. When you try it from the olster, slow down your draw in the beginning until you are consistently etting good hits on the target.

SHOOTING AT NIGHT

s a large percentage of violent crime occurs during the hours of darkness, he ability to shoot accurately at night or in bad light is very important. Unfortunately, this aspect of defensive shooting is sadly neglected, due argely to the difficulty many shooters experience in finding suitable acilities for night shooting. Nevertheless, there is still a fair amount that an be done to learn night shooting even if a suitable range cannot be found.

The amount of light that will be available at night varies. In a brightly lit treet, visibility may be so good that the firing of an aimed shot is possible. The other extreme is where it is so dark that the target is barely visible or annot be seen at all. There is also the possibility that the shooter himself nay have a torch which he can use to illuminate the target. Obviously, it s in the areas of shooting in bad light where the sights cannot be used, as vell as the use of a torch, that training and practice are most needed.

In circumstances where you do not have a torch and the light is so bad hat the sights are useless, very good results can be obtained up to about five netres by using the hip shooting method where the gun is pushed well out n front of you. Shooting becomes difficult at those ranges where the pistol vould normally be aimed; but, provided you have done your homework nd practised some instinctive shooting using a two-handed shooting posi- ion, success will be much easier. You will have to try to duplicate your wo-handed instinctive shooting in darkness and this is not so easy. In laylight, even though you are not using the sights, when you look over the istol at the target, your eyes still can see the barrel. The fact that you can see the pistol out of the corner of your eye helps guide it on to the target. This does not occur in bad light, except when shooting from the hip; consequently you tend to try to look for the pistol, often bringing it up too high. Most shots fired at night tend to go high for this reason, so deliberately point the pistol low when using either one of the two-handed holds. With a revolver, the locked, two-handed straight arms stance is very effective, probably because the pull in the shoulders is a good guide as to when you are in the right position. The Weaver stance needs a little more practice.

A good method of learning to shoot at night is to dry shoot in a darkened room. By freezing in the position you have taken after pulling the trigger and by having someone turn on the lights, you can see where the shot would have gone.

Where a torch is used it is advisable to have both the front and rear sights painted with a white dot and bar respectively so that they can be easily seen.

You can do this easily yourself with model paint.

The danger of using a torch is that you could give your position away to your assailant. The chances of this happening can be considerably reduced if you adopt the one-handed shooting stance or shoulder point position and hold the torch well away with the free hand.

This can be varied by dropping into the kneeling position, still keeping the torch away from the body.

At the closer ranges, where some speed is necessary, you can shine the beam from the torch directly at your attacker to try to blind him. Further back, the illumination of the sights is probably more important and the light from the torch should be directed so that you can see the sights, not the target. The ability to aim the torch is, perhaps, just as important as aiming the gun, so plenty of practice with both is required. You may find it better to hold the torch with the thumb placed on the inside and engage the light button with the middle finger. Flashes of light are directed at the target, not a constant beam, and you must practise changing your position after each shot.

If range facilities are available for night shooting, *take extra care, particularly when loading and making safe*. The Range Officer should check the condition of each shooter's handgun using a torch, before and after shooting. In the initial stages of shooting without sights, it helps if you freeze in your position after firing and have someone shine a torch on you so that you can check just where the pistol is pointing. This is of great assistance if you have missed as you know what correction has to be made.

While night shooting is probably one of the most difficult aspects of defensive pistol shooting, it can be mastered with an intelligent approach and practice.

Shooting at Moving Targets

One of the difficulties of defensive shooting is that the assailant is invariably moving when being shot at or in the process of attacking you. At the closer ranges, the fact that your attacker is moving should not be much of a problem, but it will become increasingly difficult to score hits at the longer

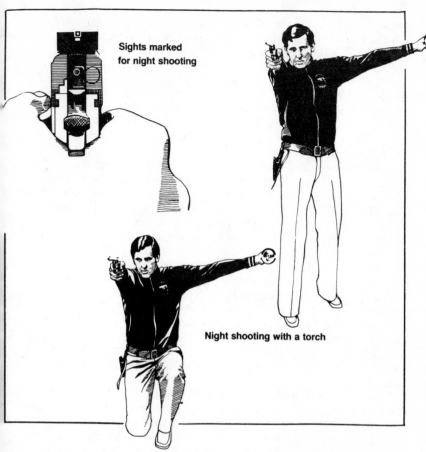

Sights marked for night shooting

Night shooting with a torch

ranges. At most distances there is no need to aim off in front of a moving target, although you may have to do this if the range is more than 25 yards. When engaging moving targets at ranges over 10 yards, swing and follow the target, firing as you start to overtake it.

Shooting at moving targets is another aspect of defense shooting that is neglected, although this is understandable because of the difficulty of constructing suitable targets. A fairly easy moving target can be made with a small cart with wheels or a sledge. The target is placed on this and two stakes are driven into the ground some distance apart on either side of the sledge. A hank of rope is tied to either end of the sledge and passed around each stake so that someone standing just behind you can pull the rope towards him, moving the sledge towards the stake. Its direction of travel can be altered by pulling the other rope passed around the other stake.

Long Range Defensive Shooting

Until now, a great deal of emphasis has been placed on the need to be able to shoot quickly and accurately at close quarters. Although most pistol fights are at short distances, there is no guarantee at what range you can expect to have to shoot in defense of your life. An exception is home defense, where the length of a room or passage will probably be the maximum distance involved. Although designed for close range, handguns can be shot accurately at distances much greater than most people think possible. A good example of what can be done with a handgun in the hands of an expert is an incident involving a team of United States Border Patrol Officers who, armed only with .38 Special revolvers, became engaged in a gunfight with smugglers, one of whom was shooting at them with a rifle about 200 yards away. While the other members of the team dealt with the smugglers closer to hand, one of the Patrolmen, Sam McKone, took on the rifleman with his revolver. In the course of the battle McKone, scored three hits on the rifleman. Sam McKone was an outstanding pistol shot, holding many awards but, by any standards, his battle with the rifleman was exceptional shooting. The chances of having to shoot at ranges above 60 yards using a handgun are unlikely and the most likely range would probably be between 15 yards and 40 yards.

Two aspects have to be considered when shooting at ranges of above 15 yards. It is most important to hit your adversary as quickly as you can which, because of the distance involved, is difficult. Secondly, where possible you should reduce the chances of your being hit by either presenting a smaller target to your attacker or making use of available cover. The technique of shooting at long range has already been covered in aiming and trigger control, which become critical the further away your target is although some of the shooting positions that will be described will assist in achieving greater accuracy.

Where you are caught in the open with no cover immediately to hand, there are two actions you can take. By assuming a prone position on the ground you will make yourself a small target and be in an accurate shooting position. When bullets start flying around you will hit the deck without hesitation, ignoring grazed knees and elbows; but it is important to learn how to go down without shooting yourself.

The prone position can be quickly assumed by sinking down on your knees where, if still in the holster, the pistol is drawn. As you fall forward push the gun out in front of you and break your fall with the other hand, rolling on the shoulder of the shooting arm.

If your weapon is a single action automatic, dis-engage the safety when you are fully prone. There are two methods of lying, the simplest being to push both arms straight out in front of you to grip the pistol. This has the disadvantage of being uncomfortable because the head must be forced back, placing strain on the neck muscles. This can be avoided by resting the side of your head on the shoulder of the shooting arm.

Once in the prone position, you can move to cover or change your position by simply rolling in either direction. If your gun is already in your hand when you go to the ground, keep it pointed well in front of you to avoid accidents.

Shooting from a kneeling position has a number of advantages even though more of the body is exposed. It is useful to use from a position of

cover, such as behind a wall or over the hood of a motor vehicle; and, because it can be quickly assumed, it permits the shooter to move his position if required. The kneeling position which provides the most flexibility of movement is dropped into by simply taking a fairly big step forward, taking the body weight on that knee which is on the same side as your shooting hand. If the pistol is holstered, it should be drawn as the knee touches the ground. Either the straight arm or Weaver type hand holds can be used from this position.

The other position takes longer to get into and, while not so flexible, provides a firmer base from which to shoot. Here you sit back on the heel of the knee which is on the ground, resting the elbow of the supporting hand on top of the other one.

The value of shooting from the several seated positions is questionable. It takes longer to get into or move from being seated and the only advantge would appear to be that a firmer shooting position can be obtained. The best seems to be where the knees are drawn up to the body and the elbows of both arms are placed inside the legs. If there is some support against which the back can be rested, a very strong shooting position can be obtained.

Whenever one is shot at from some distance away, cover should be resorted to if it is available. Cover can either be that which obscures you from the vision of your assailant, or something that will give protection against high velocity bullets. The walls of most buildings will give this protection, but be wary of interior walls in modern buildings. While these may appear substantial, they are often simply dividers constructed of wood and board. A motor vehicle can also be used to hide behind, provided you put the engine block area between you and your attacker. Almost all high velocity rifle bullets as well as some pistol ammunition, such as the magnums, will penetrate both sides of the passenger compartment of a motor vehicle.

Several methods of shooting from behind cover, such as a wall, were developed by the American Federal Bureau of Investigation and these are now used by many Police Forces in the United States. The positions permit shooting while standing or kneeling, expose very little of the shooter's body and provide a firm base from which to fire. These techniques are best suited for revolvers, for which they were designed, but have one disadvantage in that the weak hand must be used to grip the pistol on occasions.

To take up a position behind cover when standing, place your hand gripping the pistol just forward of the edge of the wall. Then support the wrist between the thumb and fingers of the other hand, placing the palm flat against the back of the wall.

You can obtain a very strong hold if you use the alternative method of gripping the wrist of the shooting arm with the free hand. The arm of the supporting hand is then placed against the wall. Regardless of which method you use, make sure that the gun does not come in contact with the side of the wall.

Use the same eye as the hand holding the pistol to aim with and stand with the foot of the inside leg placed forward.

When kneeling, the position of the hands is the same as just described

Kneeling position

Seated position

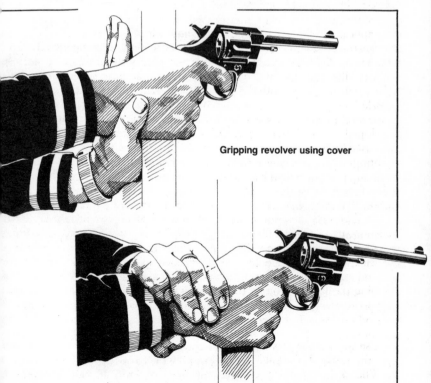

Gripping revolver using cover

93

while your body weight is placed on the outside knee. Once again, use the same eye as the hand holding the handgun to aim with.

Both these positions demand the use of the hand closest to the corner of the wall to grip the pistol, so depending upon which side of cover you have to shoot, you may have to use your weak hand. If you are using an automatic, do not use the method where the wrist is gripped by the free hand as there is a danger of it being struck by the slide or hammer during firing.

A method that is suited for revolvers and automatics alike, provides flexibility and allows you to use the strong hand to hold the pistol, irrespective of which side of a wall you are shooting from, is just to stand or kneel behind cover using one of the two–handed shooting methods. Where the cover allows you to stand with your shooting hand exposed, the Weaver stance can be used to advantage but has the disadvantage of exposing more of you when firing from the opposite side. You can reduce this by using the outside eye to aim with.

If you are using something like a wall as cover you can vary your position by standing and kneeling as you shoot. By doing this when you are being shot at, your adversary will never know the exact position you will next appear to return his fire. Not only will you reduce the chances of being hit, but you will be in a better chance to wrest command of the situation by catching your attacker off balance.

Reloading Under Fire

The need for reloading when shooting in self-defense is comparitively rare. This is most likely because the majority of battles with handguns are at close range and are usually decided, one way or another, after two or three shots have been fired. It is a mistake to adopt a dogmatic stand on this, however, as most handguns have only a limited ammunition capacity, and there is the possibility of having to reload in a protracted gunfight, particularily if it is at long range. In such circumstances there is a very real need to conserve ammunition by making every shot count. In the excitement it is very easy to blaze away at nothing in particular and end up with an empty gun. This tendency can be curbed by learning to count how many shots have been fired until it becomes a habit. In this way you should be able to avoid suddenly finding that all your ammunition has been expended.

A revolver is slower to reload than an automatic, provided the latter has a spare loaded magazine. If the magazine is empty, the time taken in loading it with live ammunition takes longer than the recharging of a revolver cylinder. Reloading a revolver can be speeded up considerably if an efficient way of carrying spare ammunition is used. Today there are several pieces of equipment on the market such as pouches which spill five or six rounds into the hand when opened. One of the best methods of carrying spare ammunition is the old way of having leather cartridge loops stitched on to the gun belt or a holder that slips over it.

To load using this method, when the revolver is empty, transfer the gun to the weak hand, open the cylinder tipping the barrel upwards and remove the empty cases with a swift stroke of the ejector rod. If your revolver is a

Shooting from cover

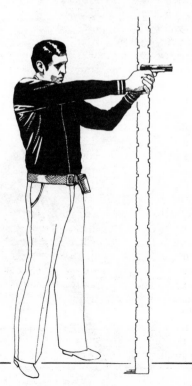

break-top design, take hold of the barrel with the other hand and point it upwards while you break it to eject the empties.

Still holding it in the weak hand, bring it down to where the cartridge loops are positioned on your belt and load the cylinder. With practice you will be able to remove two, sometimes even three rounds at a time, and load them simultaneously.

The reloading of revolvers can be speeded up almost to rival automatics if a speed or quick loader is used. These are devices, made from rubber, plastic or aluminium that hold five or six cartridges in such a position that they can be inserted simultaneously into a revolver cylinder. The first speed loader was made by Colt at the turn of the century for their first side-swing revolver but did not find favour with the shooters of that time and was discontinued. In the 1960s improved speed loaders became available and today they are very popular with a number of shooters.

Three speed loaders are commonly used at present. The simplest design consists of neoprene rubber holder that is peeled off the cartridge heads once they have been inserted in the cylinder. It provides a very fast reload

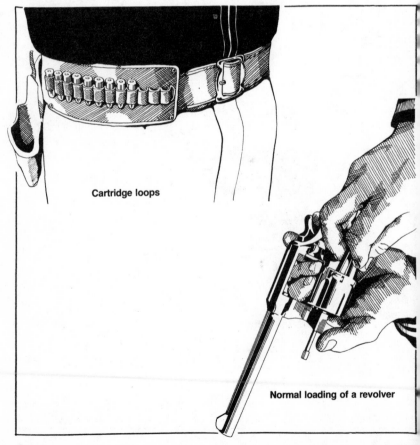

Cartridge loops

Normal loading of a revolver

Revolver Speed Loaders

1 and 2: One of the simplest speed loaders is that made by Hunt which consists of a neoprene rubber holder that is peeled off the cartridge heads once they have been inserted into the cylinder.

3 and 4: This speed loader, made by H. K. S. Tool Company, releases the cartridge heads by turning the aluminium knob, allowing them to drop into the cylinder.

4 and 5: The Matich Quick-Loader is made from tough pliable plastic and is pulled off the cartridge heads after they have been inserted into the cylinder.

but will not always retain the cartridges if accidently dropped on the ground. A modification of this model is constructed from aluminium or plastic with a button release that is either pushed or turned to release the cartridges. A completely different design consists of a strip of neoprene plastic that wraps around the back of the cartridges. When inserted into the cylinder, the strip is ripped off the cartridges. It has the advantage of holding the cartridges very securely but often tends to pull some of them out of the cylinder chambers when the strip is removed too quickly.

The method of carrying speed loaders on the belt is equally important for fast reloading. There are several designs of pouches that drop the speed loader into the hand when released but one of the simplest and best is a round loop into which the cartridges are inserted. Versions that have quick release securing catches are available as well.

To use a speed loader, first unload the revolver by transfering it to the weak hand after opening the cylinder, tip up the barrel and work the ejector rod with the thumb to eject the empty cases. While you are doing this, reach for the quick loader, which should be positioned in its holder on your belt front, and draw it out.

As you bring the quick loader up to the revolver, point its muzzle towards the ground. Slip the cartridges into the cylinder and remove the loader, allowing it to drop to the ground as you close the cylinder to resume shooting.

It has been claimed that speed loaders have little value because they are bulky to carry and will not retain the cartridges if dropped, but neither argument has much validity. Their greatest drawback is that most types will only work if round nosed ammunition is used. This means that some of the more efficient square-shouldered bullet types cannot be used. Nevertheless, speed loaders can make the revolver a much more flexible weapon.

One of the main advantages of the automatics is the ease and speed with which they can be reloaded, provided spare fully charged magazines are available. As with speed loaders, how the spare magazines are carried on the belt is important if any speed is to be attained. Very simple magazine pouches have become popular in the sport of Practical Pistol Shooting. They are an open-top design that keeps the magazine in place by friction yet provides very quick removal. While secure enough as they are, covered versions can also be obtained, although their removal for use is much slower.

Reloading an automatic involves first the removal of the empty magazine. To speed up the reload and still have a round in the chamber for emergencies, count your shots. When the last shot has entered the chamber remove the magazine. With automatics that have the button type magazine release located behind the trigger, simply depress this with your thumb dropping the empty magazine, while your free hand moves to take a loaded one from your belt.

Remove the magazine from the pouch by gripping it between the thumb and index finger so that the latter is laid along its front. This helps to guide the magazine into the butt of the pistol.

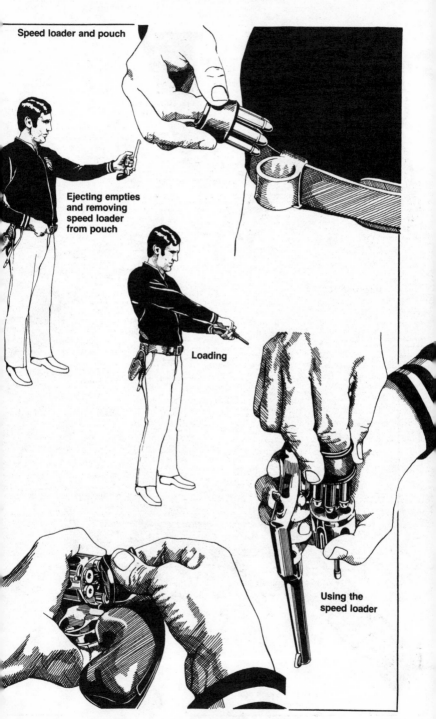

Speed loader and pouch

Ejecting empties
and removing
speed loader
from pouch

Loading

Using the
speed loader

99

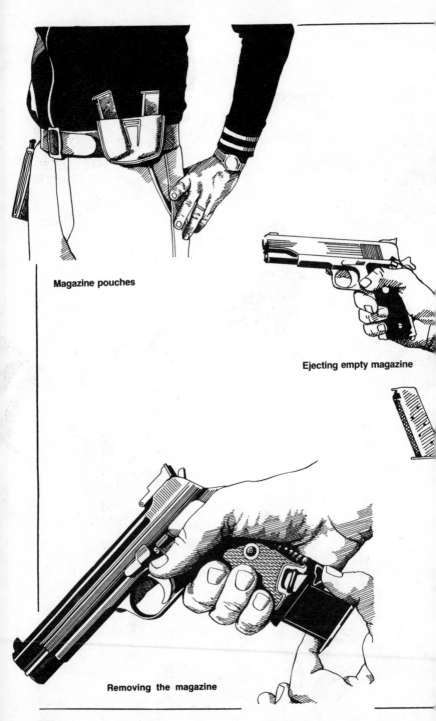

Magazine pouches

Ejecting empty magazine

Removing the magazine

100

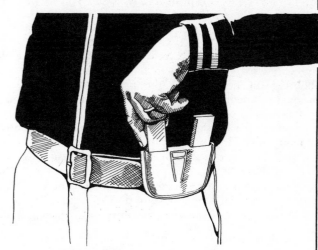

Removing loaded magazine from pouch

Inserting magazine

Bring the magazine up to the pistol and insert it, using the heel of the palm to make sure it is pushed fully home. You are now ready to resume shooting.

Combat Targets

In learning to shoot it was recommended that you use a plain, unmarked target to assist you in aiming. Similar types are used in Practical Pistol Shooting but, because the sights can be picked up so easily, you should change to something more realistic once you have attained some degree of proficiency. The most realistic combat targets are those of a fully clothed man pointing a handgun and are very good to train on because of the difficulty of picking up the sights. This type of target is not always readily available, but a good substitute can be made by painting a plain target with daubs of different coloured paint, giving it a mottled appearance. When shooting at such a target, there is no aiming mark and you must go for its centre, just as you would have to do if attacked. People have no aiming marks and the various articles of clothing worn make picking out the sights difficult.

WAX BULLETS FOR TRAINING

Learning to shoot at night or draw from the holster can be learnt with comparative safety in your home using wax bullets. This ammunition consists of a bullet made from paraffin wax, a cartridge case without powder and a primer. The explosion from the primer creates enough force to deliver the bullet with reasonable accuracy up to a range of between seven and ten metres. The velocity of the bullet is not enough to be lethal but is sufficient to cause bruising or to break the skin. While the ammunition can be used indoors using a large cardboard box stuffed with newspaper as a backstop, *the same precautions for firearms safety apply as when firing live ammunition*. A hit in the eye with a wax bullet could be very serious. Because these rounds generate no recoil they are most suited for revolvers as, with automatics, only one shot at a time can be fired. Plastic bullets, which employ the same principle are commercially available in popular revolver calibers such as 38 Special.

You can load your own wax bullets using fired cases from your pistol, provided they are of the 'Boxer' variety. 'Boxer' ammunition uses a single central flash hole (hole between primer pocket and inside of the cartridge case) which you can see by looking into a fired case. If you see only two very small holes, not a single hole in the centre, the case is of the 'Berden' type and not suitable for wax bullets. First make sure that the cases fit your gun. You may find that they have expanded during firing in which case ask a friend who reloads to resize them for you.

Remove the fired primer using a long, thin punch which has a diameter small enough to go into the flash hole. Locate the end of the punch in the flash hole, place the head of the case over a hole of a smaller diameter that has been drilled in a block of wood, and drive it out by tapping the punch with a hammer.

If a revolver is being used it is best to drill out the flash hole to a larger

Making Wax Bullets

1 and 2: Removal of fired primer.

3: Enlarging primer flash hole.

4: Using cartridge case to cut out bullet from pad of wax.

5: Seating wax bullet in bottom of case.

6: Seating fresh primer in primer pocket.

diameter using a ⅛ in (3 mm) drill. This prevents the primer from moving back and binding against the recoil plate during firing.

For bullets, you can melt either paraffin wax into a pad of about 5/16 in. thickness or use a solidified oil known as 'Toughskin' that is used to coat the tips of machine tools. This usually comes in ingots which can be sawn into the required thickness. The bullets are made by placing the open end of a primerless cartridge case on top of the pad of wax and pushing down, using the case to cut the bullet. Once the bullet has been made, use a wooden rod that will fit inside the mouth of the case to push the wax down to the bottom.

A new primer can be seated in the case head using an inexpensive priming tool that is used by reloaders. Prime your bullets only when you are going to practise as the wax can seep through the flash hole into the primer causing misfires if left for some time.

If you have your cases reloaded, KEEP THOSE USED FOR WAX BULLETS SEPARATE. A fully charged cartridge that has had the flash hole enlarged is dangerous. Also, CLEAN ALL WAX OUT OF THE BORE AND CHAMBERS *when you have finished practising*. The build up of wax in the barrel can cause bulging when normal ammunition is fired in the gun.

As mentioned at the beginning of this chapter, not everyone will need to learn all the different aspects of defensive pistol shooting that have been covered. The person who has a gun for home protection is unlikely to need to practice drawing from the holster, shooting from cover or fast reloading. On the other hand, where the gun is to be carried in a holster then probably every aspect described in this chapter should be learned.

Finally, it is not enough to learn how to shoot and then put the pistol away, never to practice again. Regular practice, even if it is mainly dry shooting or shooting with wax bullets, is needed if a handgun is to be of any use as a defense weapon.

Chapter Nine

PISTOL SHOOTING AS A SPORT

Handguns are not just for self-protection. A large number of people buy pistols solely for sport. Quite a few handgun owners, who originally wanted a handgun for protection, take up pistol shooting for recreation because they find practising with their handguns so enjoyable. The two handgun sports that have international recognition are Target Pistol Shooting and Practical Pistol Shooting. Although both sports are demanding and exciting, not every keen pistol shooter wants to become involved in competitions. Quite a few will become just 'Plinkers', which is a casual form of target shooting that uses tin cans and other small objects to shoot at. This chapter caters for those readers who are interested, or likely to become interested, in the sporting side of pistol shooting.

Target Pistol Shooting

Throughout the ages men have always prided themselves on their skill with weapons, so it is not surprising that this interest has continued since the invention of firearms. Shooting competitions with muzzle-loading long arms using circular bulls-eye targets, started as early as the 16th century in many parts of Europe. A number of quite sophisticated shooting ranges were developed, including one that featured mechanically operated moving targets. Tournaments featuring skill with firearms were also popular at fairs and festivals.

Target shooting with handguns was neglected until reliable weapons such as the revolver, were developed during the 19th century. It seems that the first organised target shooting competitions using revolvers began in England during the 1880's, when a number of pistol clubs were formed. Regular matches were held at Bisley, famous for its rifle shooting competition, while in Europe the sport was also gaining popularity, particularily in Germany and France. In America and Britain the large handgun manufacturers produced revolvers especially made for target shooting.

Surprisingly, the United States, the home of the revolver, was a late starter, with organised target competitions for handguns beginning after the turn of the century. No doubt competitions were held at town fairs and there is evidence of Wild Bill Hickok demonstrating his skill with his Navy percussion Colt Revolvers by shooting at paper targets.

Target shooting gained internationl recognition as a sport when two pistol events were included in the first Olympic Games held in Athens in 1896. The games catered for both rifle and pistol shooting and these events have been included in all subsequent Olympiads. Although there have been some changes, the two Olympic pistol matches — 'disciplines' to give them their proper title — are much as they were when first fired in Athens in 1896.

In 1907 the International Shooting Union, called simply ISU, was formed and this body now controls all international target shooting with pistol, shotgun, airgun and rifle. There are now six pistol disciplines, including the two shot in the Olympics. The ISU World Shooting Games, which are held every four years, between Olympiads, stage all six pistol disciplines. Although certain countries — America and Britain being two notable examples — have their own domestic pistol matches, the ISU disciplines are the only truly international events.

The pistols used in ISU shooting have kept pace with the sport's progress and today very accurate and sophisticated handguns are made for each discipline. These pistols have fully adjustable sights, excellent trigger pulls and grips that fit the shooter's hand like a glove. The only exception is the Center Fire match where many shooters achieve excellent results shooting the top revolvers that feature adjustable sights. The only modification to these revolvers is to equip them with the specially fitted grips like the other pistols.

Every effort at standardization of targets has been made. Except for Air Pistol, two standard targets are used for the five other disciplines. One is a circular bulls-eye target, used mainly in the precision matches, while most of the rapid fire events are shot on a large turning silhouette. Air Pistol is fired using a small reduced precision target and all three have scoring rings from one to a maximum value of ten.

Five of the disciplines are 60-shot courses, excluding sighting shots (used to adjust sights on target) while one, Air Pistol, is only 40. The maximum possible scores are 600 and 400 respectively and the ranges are 10 m for Air Pistol, 50 m for Olympic Free Pistol and 25 m for the others..

The ISU Disciplines and How to Shoot Them

Target shooting requires the mastering of all aspects of one-handed shooting that were described in Chapter Six on 'Principles of Pistol Shooting'. Equally important is an ability to overcome all nervous tension and concentrate solely on firing a perfect shot. While some of the disciplines are confined to precision shooting, others require a combination of accuracy and speed. Each discipline is a complete event in itself and, while some shooters devote all their efforts to master just one, most competitors shoot at least two if not all of them.

The Precision Matches (Air Pistol and Olympic 50 metres Free Pistol)

Air Pistol and Free Pistol are two disciplines that give the shooter plenty of time to concentrate on firing an accurate shot. Air Pistol is shot on a small reduced precision target at a range of ten metres, using one of the very accurate air or gas pistols in .177 caliber that are made especially for this event. Although these pistols are more expensive than those used by youngsters, they cost considerably less than the other target pistols. This, together with the low price of pellets and the fact that practise can be indoors makes the event an excellent method of training, although it is an international discipline. One word of warning: *the accidental discharge of an air pistol can cause serious injury,* and these handguns must be treated with the same respect as firearms.

While the range is only ten metres, shooting an air pistol is not easy. The low velocity of the pellet causes it to stay in the barrel longer than a bullet in a firearm. This means that any snatching of the trigger will result in a poor shot being fired. As it is a slow fire event, it is shot in the same manner as Free Pistol.

Fifty metres Olympic Free Pistol is, as its name implies, one of the two disciplines shot in the Olympic Games. It is fired over a distance of 50 metres on the round precision target using highly accurate .22 single shot pistols. Except for a restriction on grips, which must not support the wrist in any way, the pistols are free in the length of barrel and trigger pressures that may be used. All have sights that can be adjusted by hand, grips that fit the hand like a glove and very light hair triggers that need only the slightest touch to fire them.

A total of 60 shots to count, plus 15 sighters has to be fired within 2,5 hours. In spite of all the aids — sights, grips and light triggers — this is one of the most demanding events requiring the utmost concentration on each shot fired. As this has to be done at least 60 times the event is often described as the Pistol Shooting marathon.

In both disciplines, there is time to do everything possible to fire a perfect shot. You should prepare for each shot by checking your grip, stance and natural point of aim. Quite a few shooters mark the position of their feet once they have established their natural point of aim and, of course, grips that fit the hand like a glove help in taking the same grip every time the pistol is picked up.

Because of the long range in each event (10 metres is for an air pistol), breathing, aiming and trigger control, even with the light hair triggers, are absolutely essential for good scores. A common mistake is to shoot too fast or remain in the aim for too long, hurrying the shot when the hand starts to shake. Take your time, resting in between shots. If you do start to shake, lower the pistol and rest before trying again. It is generally agreed that the optimum time during which a shot should be fired after coming into the aim is between five and eights seconds, although this does vary with some shooters.

One principle that needs further elaboration is where to aim on the target. In target shooting the sights are not usually aligned with the centre

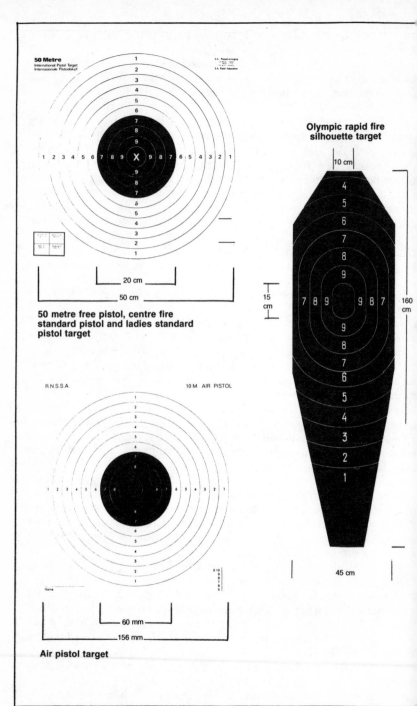

50 Metre
International Pistol Target
Internasjonale Pistolskyt

Olympic rapid fire silhouette target

50 metre free pistol, centre fire standard pistol and ladies standard pistol target

R.N.S.S.A.

10 M. AIR PISTOL

Air pistol target

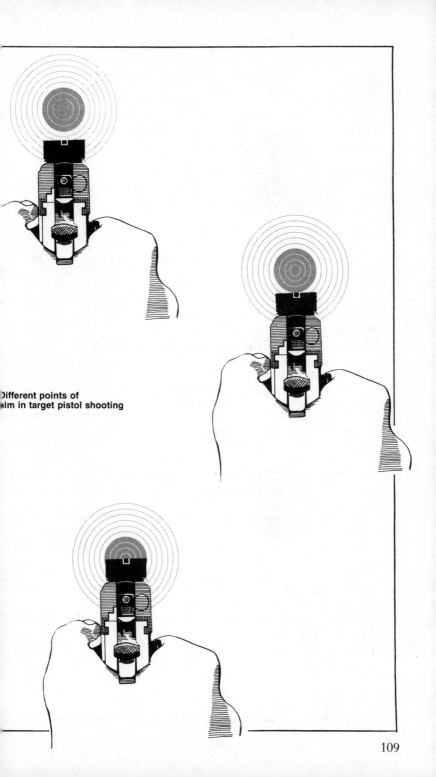

Different points of
aim in target pistol shooting

of the target, although there are some very good shooters who do this. Using the centre of the target as an aiming area is not recommended because, as was mentionėd earlier, the sights are difficult to align against the black background of the target.

A large number of shooters adjust their sights so that the center of the target will be hit when the pistol is aimed at an area below the black. This is sometimes called the 'six o'clock' hold and the black center is balanced like a ball on top of the sights. The sights can be clearly seen against the white of the target but this method also has its drawbacks. There is a tendency for the front sight to creep into the black resulting in high shots.

A number of the top shooters aim for an area below the black but leave a broad strip of white between the top of the sights and the bottom of the black.

Don't forget to aim at an area on the target rather than at a specific point. The reason for this is that nobody can keep a pistol perfectly still while aiming so, even if the sights stray slightly away from the center of the area of aim, the shot will still be a ten or a nine PROVIDED THE SIGHTS WERE KEPT PERFECTLY ALIGNED. If a specific point on the target is aimed at, there is a tendency to look through the sights at it. With practise your area of aim will slowly reduce in size.

Center Fire and Ladies Standard Pistol

Center Fire is the only event where large caliber handguns (up to a maximum of 38 or 9 mm) are used. The range is 25 metres and the match is divided into two stages, precision, which is fired on the Free Pistol Target incorporating 30 shots and five sighters and timed, or duelling, where another 30 shots are fired at the silhouette. The handguns used in this event may be either automatics or revolvers with a maximum barrel length of 153 mm (6 inches), minimum trigger pressure of 1360 grams (3 lbs) and the total weight of pistol and magazine not exceeding 1400 grams. Sights which can be adjusted using a screw driver are permitted as are the grips that are carved to fit the hand, although there are some restrictions on their width.

Ladies Standard Pistol consists of exactly the same course of fire except that .22 calibre weapons that conform with the requirements of the Standard Pistol match are used. The procedure for shooting both disciplines is the same.

In the precision stage, five sighters are permitted in eight minutes; thereafter six strings or series of five shots in six minutes are fired. As there is plenty of time for each shot, the slow fire technique used in Free pistol applies in this stage of the discipline. As a general rule, roughly one minute should be taken to fire a shot.

In the timed or duelling stage, as it is sometimes called, the shooter faces a single silhouette target that is 25 metres away. The pistol may be loaded and cocked but must be pointing at 45 degrees to the ground. When the target turns, the pistol may be raised into the aim and one shot placed on it. The silhouette faces the shooter for three seconds and turns away for seven. As with the precision stage, six series of five shots are fired with five sighters allowed prior to the commencement of the event.

To shoot this stage, prepare for each series by checking grip, stance and natural point of aim. The method of coming on to the target was described in the section 'Developing Speed' in Chapter Seven, 'Learning to Shoot'. Remember, when preparing for your shot, to follow the sights down with the eyes as you lower the pistol making sure that the sights remain correctly aligned, although the front sight will protrude above the rear when pointing at 45 degrees to the ground.

In good light you can often see the hits of previous shots on the target. This can be very distracting and can cause you to look at the target rather than the sights when you come up into the aim. To avoid doing this, fix your gaze at the bottom of the silhouette while waiting for it to turn. When it does your eyes will pick up the sights as they come up, giving you more time to align them correctly.

You must raise your pistol quickly on to the target when it turns to face you, braking your upward swing just below the centre of the silhouette. To ensure a good trigger break (pull), engage the trigger with the index finger, applying a slight amount of pressure as you wait for the target to appear. This will overcome the tendency to snatch when you are in the aim. As you start to brake near the top of your swing, increase pressure on the trigger so that the shot fires within about 2,5 to 2,8 seconds after the target turned to face you. During the seven-second wait, you should be able to take two or three breaths and, when raising the pistol, exhale. After the shot has been fired, allow for a brief follow through, then lower the pistol to 45 degrees, aligning the sights as you do so, and get ready for the next shot. If a revolver is used, it is cocked with the free hand during the seven-second interval.

Olympic Rapid Fire Pistol

Rapid Fire Pistol is the other discipline that is fired at the Olympic Games. It is a speed event that is sometimes called the 'Pistol Sprint' and, because of this, the handguns used are designed to reduce recoil to a minimum. Rapid fire pistols are specially made automatics, chambered for ,22 short and have a number of devices to help keep the movement of the gun to a minimum during firing. As with the other pistols, specially fitted grips, adjustable sights and light triggers are permissible within certain limits.

The match is divided into two identical 30-shot stages which require the shooter to engage five silhouettes at a range of 25 metres, placing one shot on each in specified time limits. Each stage consists of six five-shot series. In the first two, the targets appear for two periods of eight seconds, the time is then reduced to six seconds for the next two series and cut to four seconds for the final ones. At the commencement of each series, the shooter may be cocked and loaded but must have the pistol pointing to the ground at 45 degrees. Before the start of each stage, five sighters are allowed in any one of the time periods nominated by the shooter.

The method of firing the first shot, including preparation, is the same as for the duelling stage of Center Fire. Although opinions vary on which of the five targets one should line up on, most shooters choose the first as this is considered the most difficult to engage. If the first shot is good then, more often than not, so are those that follow. Right-handed shooters should engage the righthand target first, moving then to shoot those on the left, the reverse being the case for the left-hander or 'southpaw'.

The remaining targets are engaged by keeping the arm and shoulder locked, swinging from the hips and ankles. In the eight and six-second series there is usually time for a short follow through after a shot has been fired before swinging or turning to deal with the next one. In the four-second string, everything must be speeded up considerably and you should not worry too much about aiming at the target but rather just on keeping the sights aligned as you swing from target to target. You should try to fire the first shot in the eight second series in about 2,0 to 2,2 seconds after the targets have turned. This is reduced to 1,6 to 1,8 in the six second string and 1,1 to 1,5 seconds in the four-second ones. The targets will turn to face you approximately three seconds after you have called 'ready', so you have time for a quick breath, enabling you to exhale when you bring the pistol up on to the first target, shooting all five before taking another breath.

The secret of Rapid Fire is good nerves and confidence, making use of as much of the limited time in a series as possible. You must develop a shooting rhythm and shoot five shots evenly. In the first two series there is time for well-aimed shots on all the targets and the top shooters drop very few points here, often 'cleaning' (maximum score) all the targets. It is the four-second string that separates the good from the poor contestants. Some shooters start slowly on the first two targets and shoot the final ones slightly quicker. In all cases, the locking of the upper body during the turning movements is very important. If only the arm is used to move the pistol, the alignment of sights is disturbed in the moving from one target to another, which is fatal in the fastest series. To counteract the tendency to drop the aim on the last target, it is a good idea to move on to an imaginary sixth silhouette after all five shots have been fired.

Coming up on to the first target in the recommended time as well as developing rhythm can be very largely perfected by dry shooting. You can begin practise with live ammunition by first learning to engage the first target, then later swinging on to the next one, progressing as you improve, until you can shoot all five. Once this has been mastered, you can go on to learning to shoot first the eight-second string and then the others.

Standard Pistol

Standard Pistol is a relatively new discipline that has been modelled on one of the American domestic matches. It comprises 60 shots, fired on the 50-metre precision target at a range of 25 metres. The restrictions on the weapons used, which are invariably .22 automatics, are more stringent. The height, width and length of the pistol must be within certain measurements, while total weight of the handgun and magazine must not exceed 1 260 grams. The minimum trigger pressure allowed is 1 000 grams. Devices for reducing recoil, other than weights, are not permitted.

The match is divided into three 20-shot stages. In the precision stage, which is broken down into four identical series, a reasonable time in which to aim is allowed, although there is not sufficient to waste. Each series requires five shots to be fired in a time of 150 seconds. The time is reduced to 20 seconds a series in the timed stage and 10 seconds for the rapid. As with all the other disciplines, the shooter may be cocked and loaded before the commencement of each stage and standing with the pistol pointing at 45 degrees to the ground.

The precision stage is fired in much the same manner as that of Center Fire. Normal breathing is possible but, the shooter must try to fire two shots before lowering the pistol so that the time limit of 150 seconds is not exceeded. During a timed series, the pistol is held in the aim throughout the firing of the five shots. In the timed series, the pistol is raised as the breath is exhaled and, another breath is taken and let out between the third and fourth shots. In the rapid series, all five shots are fired on an exhaled breath and the shooting of this should be treated in the same manner as the eight-second string of Olympic Rapid Fire Pistol.

The Psychology of Target Pistol Shooting

In target competitions of the type described, success or failure depends almost as much on the psychological attitude of the shooter as it does on the ability to shoot. Many target shooters obtain excellent scores in practise yet, when faced with the tension of competition, go to pieces completely. This is to be expected with a novice. In time, he will overcome nerves and improve his match scores, but there are some shooters who have great difficulty in achieving in competitions the standard that they are capable of.

There are a number of pitfalls to avoid in the approach to target shooting. The first is to realise that, although others are competing in a competition, you are really shooting against yourself. No matter what you do, short of cheating, there is nothing you can do about the other competitors. All that you can hope for is to shoot perfect scores which nobody can beat. Learn to ignore the other shooters and the scores that they put up. Keep away from the scoreboard and concern yourself only with your own totals. Chasing scores is one way of increasing your own tension. Comparing your totals with those of others, working out how much you must score in the next stage, can really put the pressure on.

It is possible to chase scores when shooting against yourself. This often happens when you are close to bettering your previous top score, and it can be fatal to work out just how much you need to do it while shooting. It is better not to keep a running total of your score during a match which will only put the pressure on towards the end. Rather record your strikes on the target and wait until after the match to add everything up and check it against the official results on the scoreboard.

The ability to recover from a bad shot is perhaps the most difficult, even for top shooters. It is very upsetting to be shooting tens, with the odd nine and then suddenly to fire a bad shot that is a seven or worse. In a tight competition this can rarely be afforded and the temptation to give up then and there is very great.

It is important to remember that the match has not been won or lost until the last shot has been fired. While you should not concern yourself with what the other competitors are doing, there is much that can happen in

Target Handguns

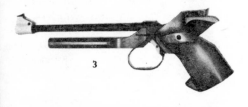

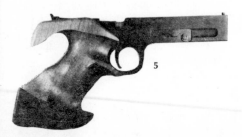

Free Pistols — 1 to 4

1 The Drulov .22 single shot pistol which is inexpensive and ideal for the novice shooter.
2 The Hammerli 120 Sport single shot pistol.
3 Hammerli's top line Free Pistol, the model 150.
4 The Russian MC 55, another top line Free Pistol.

Rapid Fire Pistols — 5 to 7.

5 The Domino Rapid Fire Pistol that is also made in .22 long rifle for Standard Pistol.

6 The Hammerli 250 Rapid Fire
  Pistol.
7 The Walther OSP Rapid Fire Pistol
  that is also made in .22 long
  rifle and .32 for Standard Pistol
  and Centre Fire respectively.

Standard Pistols — 7 to 11.
(Also suitable for Ladies
Standard Pistol.)
8 The Browning ISU .22 long rifle
  pistol.
9 The Hammerli 208 .22 long rifle
  pistol.
10 The High Standard Supermatic
  Trophy .22 long rifle pistol.

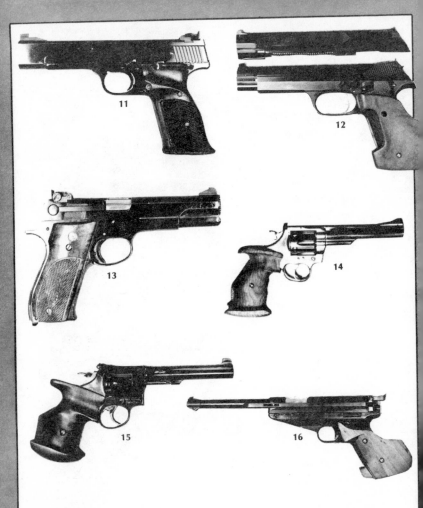

11 The Smith & Wesson Model 41
.22 long rifle pistol.

Center Fire Pistols —
12 and 13.

12 The Sig-Hammerli P 240 pistol in
38 Special with a .32 conversion unit.

13 The Smith & Wesson Model 52
in 38 Special.

Center Fire Revolvers
14 and 15

14 A Colt 357 Trooper Mark III with
6 inch (150 mm) barrel and
target grips. The Python is also
a popular target revolver when
fitted with similar grips.

15 A Smith & Wesson K 38 in 38
Special with target grips is
another very popular target revolver that can also be had in
.32.

Air Pistol — 16

16 The Feinwerkbau Model 80 .117
single shot air pistol made
especially for Target Shooting.

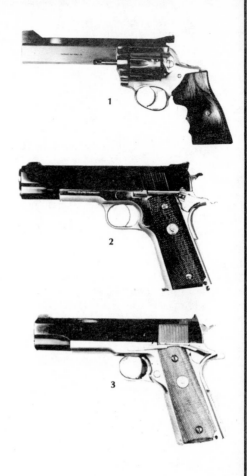

Specially Modified Handguns

1 A Ruger revolver modified for American Practical Police competitions by fitting a heavy barrel and rib with fully adjustable sights, custom grips and a light smooth double action pull.

2 A standard Colt Government 45 automatic modified by the author for Practical Pistol Shooting by extending the tang of the grip safety, fitting a Gold Cup barrel and slide with adjustable sights, grooving the front strap and main spring housing, hard chroming the frame and improving the trigger pull.

3 Another standard Colt Government 45 automatic modified for Practical Pistol Shooting by fitting adjustable sights, Barsto barrel, larger safety catch, nickeling frame and improving the trigger pull.

a competition and many a good shooter has carried the day even though a shot was dropped in a match.

The only real way to discipline yourself to recover is to treat every single shot, even when fired in timed events, as a match in itself. Learn to concentrate solely on the shot you are firing and ignore what has happened before or what is to come. This also helps your concentration and is something every shooter must strive for. As your shooting and ability to recover improve you will find that dropped shots decrease or become eights and nines instead of sevens and sixes.

Conclusion

The only other item of necessary equipment is a good spotting scope to look at the strikes on your target. Most target shooters invest in a pistol box to carry all their handguns and equipment and it certainly is an asset. Other items such as shooting glasses or iris apertures can be considered at a later stage.

Finally, a question that is often asked is: 'How does one start Target Pistol Shooting?' A complete answer is difficult to give. Not only are the handguns expensive but none of the disciplines can be classed as easy. For the shooter with a suitable defense handgun, such as a revolver, the answer is simple—the Center Fire match is the only one that can be considered. But what about those who want to start target shooting from scratch?

Perhaps the best advice is that given by a very fine South African ISU shooter, Trevor Hull. He maintains that a beginner should first invest in a pistol suitable for the Standard Pistol and learn to shoot, not only this discipline, but also Free Pistol and Rapid Fire. Shooting a standard pistol in either of these matches is quite permissible and, once reasonable scores are being achieved, the novice will be in a far better position to know what weapons will suit him best for these disciplines. This is very sound advice and probably the best way to start ISU shooting.

Practical Pistol Shooting

Practical Pistol Shooting is relatively new to the international sporting scene, the first world championships having being held in Switzerland as recently as 1975. The sport is becoming increasingly popular in Western Countries and, as its name suggests, is closely aligned to defensive pistol shooting.

The origins of Practical Pistol Shooting go back to before the second World War when, in America, the Federal Bureau Of Investigation had just been authorised to arm its agents. At that period the Bureau, which had been reorganised by its director, J. Edgar Hoover, was in the process of stamping out the last vestiges of violent crime that had flourished during the days of prohibition. With F.B.I. agents frequently in danger of being involved in shootouts with criminal elements, the need for good, realistic firearms training was apparent.

In addition to the other firearms used, the Bureau designed a training course for revolvers which they called their Practical Pistol Course. This was used for basic training and is now used in similar form by many other

118

Police Forces in America. The course provides for the trainees to fire, using cover in some cases, at various distances that range between seven yards and 50 yards. During the course the shooter has to use most of the positions that have been described in Chapter Eight on 'Defensive Pistol Shooting' as well as reloading. Although many experts maintain that the course is too easy, when considered for what it is, namely, a basic training course, it still has much to commend it.

In the '60s, State and National Combat Pistol competitions became popular with American Police Forces and the F.B.I. Practical Pistol Course was adopted as a basis for these matches. Today, the matches are very popular but, as with most sports, the competitive spirit and desire to win of the shooters has tended to rob the competition of much of its previous practical usefulness. Competitors now use revolvers that have been extensively modified with heavy barrels to reduce recoil and worked over double action triggers that almost rival a good single action pull. These are not the handguns that the competitors carry when on duty and the sport has been described as little more than 'a glorified double action target match'. While it is true that it is no longer very practical as a means of training it is, of course, now a sport and must be treated as such.

These revolver combat matches are restricted solely to members of Police Forces and law enforcement agencies in America. For a long time civilian shooters in that country were restricted to participating in Target competitions but, about the same time as combat shooting was gaining popularity with the police, so a small band of civilian shooters in California was developing its own form of combat shooting. Under the leadership of Jeff Cooper, a very good pistol shooter and well known gun writer, much experimentation with different techniques and weapons was carried out. Starting in small ways, and largely due to the efforts of Jeff Cooper, the sport spread to other parts of the world. In 1976 the International Practical Shooting Confederation was formed to regulate the sport on an international scale. The name of the sport, which had been originally called 'Combat Pistol Shooting' was changed to 'Practical Pistol Shooting' and world championships are now held every two years.

To describe the form that Practical Pistol Shooting takes is difficult because no standard courses exist as in Target Pistol Shooting. The idea is to design a different course of fire for each competition to provide shooting variety and also realism because, in a real life situation, there are no standard incidents. As few restrictions as possible are placed on the weapons and equipment competitors may use.

Any revolver or automatic may be used, provided it is chambered for a minimum caliber of .38 Special and 9 mm respectively. Spare magazines and quick loaders may be carried and speed holsters that permit a very fast draw are permitted if they can hold the handgun securely when the competitor is running or climbing during some of the courses that are fired. A very simple figure target with a plain, light-coloured background is used. There are no aiming marks on it except two central scoring rings that are hardly visible.

A hit in the central ring scores maximum points, irrespective of the caliber of handgun used, but shots on the remainder of the target are scored depending upon the caliber. Major calibers of 41 and above as well as the 357 Magnum score higher values than the minor 38 Special or 9 mm parabellum. This is because it is felt that the major calibers have more stopping power and therefore warrant higher points.

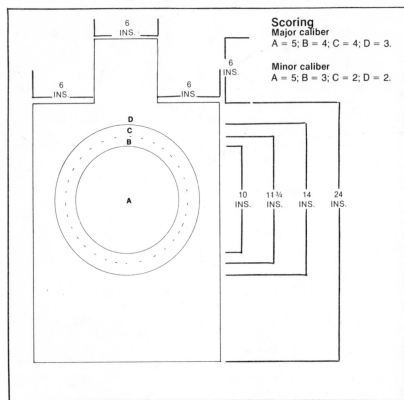

Scoring

Major caliber
A = 5; B = 4; C = 4; D = 3.

Minor caliber
A = 5; B = 3; C = 2; D = 2.

Today the most popular handguns are single action automatics such as the .45 Colt Government Model and the 9 mm Browning High Power. These handguns are often extensively modified and improved and, for accuracy, rival some of the best target pistols.

In almost every case, a stage in a competion starts with the pistol holstered. While the techniques used in shooting are the same as those that have been described in Chapter Nine, drawing from a speed holster needs some additional explanation. These holsters have a front rake that cants the butt of the handgun rearwards permitting a very fast draw and providing some measure of safety in that the muzzle of the pistol points towards the target.

The basic principles of drawing from the holster still apply but the shooter commences by standing with his hands clasped in front of him or raised at shoulder height in the surrender attitude. On the command to fire,

**The Practical
Pistol Draw**

the shooting hand goes straight to the holster and grips the pistol butt, thumb ready, but not on the safety catch. The pistol is drawn backwards until it clears the holster and then thrust forward towards the target. If a two-handed hold is to be used, the remainder of the draw is as described in 'Drawing a Single Action Action Automatic' in Chapter Nine.

Apart from being able to draw from the holster, quick magazine changing is also an essential. The most popular two-handed shooting position used in this sport is the Weaver stance and, as automatics are invariably used, it is particularily suited for this type of shooting.

Although there are no laid down shooting events, most competitions have a 'Standard Exercises' shoot and a 'Jungle Lane' or an 'Assault Course' included in their course of fire. The former is a series of different exercises at varying ranges usually involving drawing from the holster and engaging the target with a specified number of shots within a time limit, the latter events provide the competitor with a situation in which he must engage a number of targets. The shooter is usually required to move to various positions from which he must shoot. These events are scored by taking the shooter's score and dividing it by the time he took to complete the course.

While the basic principles of shooting apply, there are a few additional techniques that can be used to good effect. In the Standard Exercises, for example, it pays to prepare yourself by establishing your natural point of aim before you holster the gun. In the assault course shoots you should carefully study where the targets are placed and work out just where you will reload or change magazines. When doing so, remember to count your shots so that you always have a round in the chamber when you change a magazine. Also, try to reload or change magazines when you move between shooting positions so that you can save as much time as possible.

Practical Pistol Shooting has not escaped criticism, the most voluble being that it is no longer practical. When one sees some of the modifications to the pistols and the type of holsters used, this is fair comment. Nevertheless, it is a sport that is probably closer to the realities of defensive shooting than any other and, apart from that, is both exciting and enjoyable. It is unfortunate that it is becoming more confined to the use of the single action automatic, tending to exclude all other handgun types.

In conclusion, because of the handguns used and the type of shooting, this is not a sport that should be attempted until the beginner has mastered all the aspects of defensive shooting. Any person who takes up this sport must intend to become an expert in both the handling and shooting of a pistol.

Chapter Ten

ACCESSORIES AND MODIFICATIONS

Provided you have chosen wisely, there should be no real need to have your handgun modified or altered. You should be able to learn to handle and shoot without much difficulty any well-made pistol of good design that suits your particular needs. Nevertheless, it is almost impossible for any gun manufacturer to design a handgun that will suit everyone perfectly. Just the many differences in the anatomy of individual human beings is enough to defeat the most ingenious gun designer so, in the end, the best that can be hoped for is a compromise that suits the majority of shooters' needs reasonably well.

It is not uncommon for handgun enthusiasts to have their guns extensively modified, regardless of the expense involved. Few owners who have bought a pistol for defence will wish to go to such extremes. Nevertheless, after learning to shoot, they may find that their guns have some minor shortcomings that can be rectified with a few inexpensive modifications.

Handgun Grips

Handgun grips or stocks, as they are sometimes called, very often leave much to be desired and few production guns, especially revolvers, fit the individual hands of shooters well. This is probably the most difficult task facing a handgun manufacturer as the hands of different people vary so much in size and shape that even a good compromise is difficult to achieve. Fortunately, there are now a large range of custom grips made for the more popular makes. These are reasonably priced and it should be possible to find one that will improve the handguns grip considerably.

Handguns that are intended to be used purely for defence need grips that are comfortable to hold; point the gun naturally at the target; are able to absorb recoil without disturbing the shooter's hold; and correctly position the index finger on the trigger so that the pull will be straight to the rear.

An examination of revolver grips indicates that those of the old Colt single actions fitted most hands pretty well which is one of the reasons why

Grips

1 Standard grips of Colt Trooper Mrk III recarved and finished by author.
2 Modified Jordan style grips carved by author for custom 45 Colt revolver.
3 Herrett stocks fitted to Smith & Wesson Model 19 Combat Magnum revolver.
4 Herrett stocks fitted to Colt Detective Special revolver.

5 Pachmayr rubber grips fitted to Colt Python revolver.
6 Pachmayr rubber grips fitted to Smith & Wesson Model 60 Chiefs Special.
7 Pachmayr rubber grips fitted to Colt 45 Government Model.
8 Pachmayr rubber grips fitted to a Browning Hi-Power 9 mm.

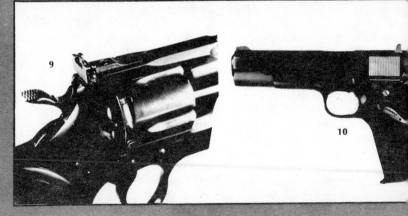

Sights

9 Top grade revolvers, like the Colt Python, are usually fitted with excellent sights that are fully adjustable.

10 This Colt Government 45 automatic has been fitted with improved sights that have a higher profile.

11 Fully adjustable sights like this one by MMC are easy to install on automatics as they are made to fit the dovetail recess in the frame that holds the existing sight. Similar such sights are made by Bomar and Micro.

12 Many practical pistol shooters have Smith & Wesson fully adjustable revolver sights fitted to their automatics as illustrated by this Colt Government 45 belonging to the author. This conversion involves a considerable amount of accurate machining and is expensive.

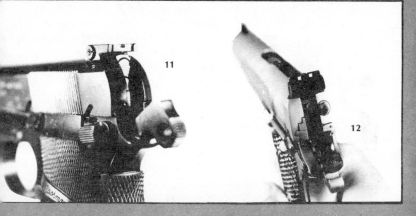

this handgun continued to be popular long after double actions had been introduced. The modern double action revolver stocks are not as good, having two main faults. The angle between the barrel and the stock is about 15 degrees compared with 20 for the single action, which is the main reason why this latter gun points more naturally at the target. More serious is the gap between the rear of the trigger guard and the front strap under which the third or middle finger should rest. This usually places the index finger too high to engage the trigger comfortably and can also allow the gun to move in the hand when heavy loads (powerful ammunition) are fired.

An early attempt to solve these problems were grip adaptors which were made by Frank Pachmayr of America who is now famous for his handgun grips and pistol-smithing. The adaptors were plastic inserts that clipped on to the front part of the metal of the grip, being held in place by the normal wooden stocks. This adaptation helped fill the troublesome gap behind the rear of the trigger guard and also improved the stock-to barrel angle. Aesthetically, they did little to enhance the appearance of the gun, but they were effective and improved revolver grips considerably. The adaptors were first introduced before the Second World War and are still available for most of the popular makes of the revolver.

The revolver makers have themselves attempted to improve the grips of some of their models. Just before the Second World War, Smith & Wesson made special oversize target stocks for their K series revolvers that were modelled on similar stocks designed by custom grip maker Walter Roper. These stocks completely encased in wood the metal at the front of the grip and filled the gap behind the trigger guard. They were a great improvement and were so popular that Smith & Wesson now offer a number of their revolvers with these. Colt followed suit after the war, fitting grips of similar design to their top revolvers and a number of other makers offer some of their products with stocks of the same type. Colt have recently also improved the grips of their small-framed short barrel revolvers, such as the Cobra and Detective Special, by equipping them with excellent combat-style grips.

Good though the oversize target stocks on the bigger revolvers are, they are not perfect. Quite often they are too large to hold in complete comfort, although this can be rectified if you are prepared to modify the grips yourself. If you have any woodworking ability, this can be done quite easily with a knife and file. Once shaped to suit your hands, the grips can be sanded and either varnished or polished to restore their appearance. Of course the diamond checkering will have to be removed in the process, but this is not critical. Many consider that smooth grips are ideal for defence use as they allow quick adjustments to be made when drawing from the holster.

In addition to what has been described, there are now very large selections of custom grips designed to fit most hands and made for almost all of the well-known revolvers. Such stocks, made by firms like Herrett, Fitz and Mustang, are all good designs while Frank Pachmayr produces a whole range of neoprene rubber grips for revolvers.

Very good revolver combat grips, known as the Jordan Trooper, are made by Herretts. These follow the design of Bill Jordan, a United States

Border Patrolman who has had many years of shooting experience in law enforcement and is one of the greatest living double action revolver exponents. His design covers both the front and back of the metal of the grip in wood which assists in absorbing the heavy recoil of magnum ammunition. The grips are smooth and comfortable to hold, particularily for shooters with large hands.

Although the grips of the first automatics were atrocious, those of most of the modern self-loaders suitable for defence shooting are superior to double action revolvers. With exceptions, automatics — even those chambered for the big calibres — are comfortable to hold. The exceptions are those automatics that have large magazine capacities, such as the 9 mm Browning Hi-Powers. Because of having to double stack a large number of rounds in the magazine, the stock to barrel angle is often poor and, in the case of this particular handgun, the tang at the top of the frame is very short and can cause the web of the hand to be pinched by the hammer during firing.

Practical Pistol Shooters often modify their automatics extensively, including the grips. Most of these modifications involve work on the metal rather than on the wood stocks. The tangs can be built up with a weld to give more protection to the web of the hand while the metal front of the grips is heavily checkered or stippled to prevent movement in the hand during firing. Some shooters, who like to curl the finger of the supporting hand around the front of the trigger guard, have it straightened or dished to provide a better hold.

While all these modifications are very nice, they are also expensive and not really necessary for the average shooter. Wooden grips with built in thumb rests are available and, once again, Frank Pachmayr produces a fairly wide range of his rubber grips that wrap around the front of the metal of the gun, giving a similar effect to checkering. In the case of the .45 Colt Government Automatic, the size of the grip can be easily altered by fitting either the arched or straight mainspring housing into the rear of the frame.

Good grips are very important to the target shooter who is striving to hit the central ring with every shot. To help achieve this, well designed target stocks that fit the shooter's hand like a glove are needed to enable the same grip to be taken every time the pistol is picked up. With the exception of the Center Fire revolvers, which need to have special grips fitted, all the handguns designed for target shooting have stocks with built in thumb rests and adjustable heel platforms. Most also have a generous amount of wood that can be removed by the shooter so that he can modify the grips to suit his hand.

In conclusion, it must be stressed that no modifications to the grips of a new handgun should be made when it is first acquired. It would be quite wrong to pretend that new stocks are required for every pistol. The standard factory grips may well be quite adequate, if not perfect, for accurate shooting. The fitting of custom grips to a handgun should only be considered after its owner has learnt to shoot it as only then will he, or she, have any idea of what is needed. Good handgun grips are only an aid to a good shooter but will do nothing for a poor shot. Accuracy with a pistol, in the end, depends upon the man, or the woman, behind the gun.

Sights

With the continual emphasis that has been placed on aiming in the earlier pages of this book, it follows that good pistol sights are a must and should be an important consideration when choosing any automatic or revolver.

Early shoulder and hand-held firearms were inherently inaccurate over any distance and, consequently few, if any, had devices for aiming. In time, as guns improved in reliability and accuracy, the need to be able to aim resulted in sights being fitted to pistols and shoulder weapons. Most sights of the early weapons were crude and even those of the early Colt revolvers, which themselves were quite capable of delivering good accuracy, left much to be desired. These old Colts had a front sight consisting of a small brass post while the rear was simple a V filed into the hammer. The guns could be aimed only when cocked and any play in the hammer did little to assist accuracy.

The greatest improvements in sights has been though Target Pistol Shooting. Starting with the early weapons produced in the late 1880s, pistol sights have been improved until, today, many handguns have them of excellent quality and design. Experimentation with the design of sights has established that the best are those of the partridge type which consist of a square-shouldered front sight blade with a rectangular notch in the rear leaf. In service handguns, the front sight must be ramped at the back if the gun is to be carried in a holster. Target shooters prefer the front sight to be square or undercut at the rear so that it is easy to see. When aligned, the sights must be big enough to see easily and there must be enough light visible on either side of the front sight to assist in ensuring that it is placed in the centre of the rear notch.

Of modern handguns, the sights of well made revolvers are, generally speaking, very good. Those with fixed sights are of the Partridge variety and are large and easy to pick up during fast shooting. The top grade revolvers are often fitted with fully adjustable rear sights which enable them to be used for both defence and target shooting.

The sights of automatics vary from good to poor. While a number of good quality self-loaders are made in Europe, with good sights, quite a few still have sights that are small and difficult to pick up. Two of the worst offenders are the Browning Hi-Power 9 mm and the Colt .45 Government Model which, although excellent handguns in all other respects, have sights which can best be described as average. With the former, the front sight is too thin, while the Colt's has a very low profile. Some automatics, the Colt Gold Cup (A target version of the Government model) and a sporting version of the 9 mm Browning, have excellent adjustable sights.

Where a handgun— one of the older revolvers or an automatic — has poor sights, better ones can often be fitted by a good gunsmith. For those of the fixed variety, the cost need not be great and many gunsmiths vastly improve a handgun by just putting on a set of good sights.

Many practical pistol shooters have fully adjustable rear sights fitted to their automatics. Depending upon the sight used and how it is fitted, this modification can be very successful and will greatly improve the accuracy of the pistol. One has to be careful when doing this, however, as some sights tend to shake loose when the slide slams back and forth during firing.

For night shooting, it helps to have a white dot in the centre of the front sight face and a white bar just under the rear notch. This does not necessarily help you see the sights in the dark but illuminates them when a torch is used. Many Continental automatics are being produced with sights of this type although, with a little white paint, an artist's brush, and a steady hand, there is no reason why the shooter cannot do this himself. In the United States some companies modify existing sights with a luminous bars and dots that enables them to be picked up at night without a torch.

The sights on a good target handgun are excellent and require no modifications. While these types of sights are obviously essential for target shooting, what is their value in defence shooting? For the shooter who intends buying his ammunition over the counter, probably very little. Fixed sights have the advantage of being very robust and will not be damaged should the gun be dropped nor will they shake loose during firing. These guns are pre-sighted at the factory and are good enough for any defence situation. On the other hand, the target sights on revolvers, and some automatics, are also strongly constructed and, because they are adjustable, can help deliver the bullet to the target with more accuracy. Having sights that can be adjusted to suit your eyes is definitely an advantage, especially if you reload your own ammunition, as they can then be zeroed (adjusted) for different cartridge loadings.

Good sights are an asset to accurate shooting and, if those on your weapon are not of the best, it is worthwhile seeing if they cannot be improved at reasonable cost.

Triggers and Safeties

A trigger with a good crisp pull is another aid to good shooting. The best single action pulls in a defense handgun should need a pressure of between 3 to 5 lbs (1,36 kg to 2,27 kg) to set them off. A double action pull must be as smooth as possible and not too heavy.

Target weapons, naturally enough, have excellent trigger pulls with those of Free Pistols only needing a pressure of a few grams to fire them. The top quality revolver triggers are equally as good, both on single and double action. Even so, while the double action pulls of Colt and especially Smith & Wesson revolvers are very good, they can be considerably improved by a pistolsmith who knows what he is doing. That of a Colt can be made very much smoother while some of the initial hardness of the Smith & Wesson pull can be lightened.

With exceptions, the trigger pull of many automatics is not quite so good. On single action, their triggers often have a lot of creep or drag before the hammer falls, unlike the crisp pull of a good revolver. Double action triggers of automatics rarely rival those of top quality revolvers, being either too heavy or too rough. Nevertheless, while not as good, most well-made automatics have triggers that are good enough for the average user. Only if you want to take up pistol shooting seriously, need you worry unduly about the trigger.

Most of the custom work on guns these days is done on the automatics used by Practical Pistol shooters. In addition to having a trigger job done, the pistols are fitted with larger, easier to operate safeties. While not so critical on a Colt, this is very necessary on the Browning 9 mm High Power, because of its very small safety-catch. Other modifications are the polishing of the feed ramp as well as the chamfering of the edges of the magazine well to make the insertion of the magazine easier and faster.

While it is possible for a home gunsmith to do some of these modifications, *they are best left to a good professional who knows what he is doing.* Trying to improve triggers can often lead to making the weapon *unreliable or even unsafe.* Where modifications to safety catches and magazine releases are carried out, *make quite sure that there is no chance that these can be moved or operated while in the holster.* Quite a few shooters remove the magazine safety from the Browning Hi Power. This device, which prevents the gun from being fired with the magazine removed, is often seen to serve little purpose by some and its removal can improve the trigger. The desirability of this modification is really up to the individual but one alteration that is *not recommended is the tying down or pinning of the grip-safety on a Colt 45 Automatic.* This device, which permits the handgun to fire only when properly gripped, is a safety measure well worth keeping in a pistol of this type.

Trigger pressures on target guns, good as they are, can sometimes be improved by the fitting of a trigger shoe, a small fitting that is clamped on the front of the trigger using Allen screws. It gives the trigger finger a greater area to engage. *Great care must be taken if these are fitted to automatics that will be carried as the shoe can come in contact with the leather of the holster causing the pistol to fire.*

It is probably true to say that few modifications, if any, need be contemplated by the average shooter, provided he has a well-made handgun. The easiest modification is the fitting of new grips which is often well worth the expense. Still, it is always worth bearing in mind that a good pistol can be made even better with a few sensible modifications and alterations, if the shooter is prepared for the additional expense.

Chapter Eleven

CARE AND CLEANING

A good quality handgun should last a lifetime, perhaps even several lifetimes, provided it is properly maintained. The most important reason for keeping a handgun in tip-top condition, particularly if it is for defence purposes, is to prevent malfunctions. Equally important is the fact that *careless handling or neglect* can ruin an expensive automatic or revolver, *to a point where it becomes dangerous to use*.

Handgun Care

It is reasonable to expect a handgun to pick up a few surface scratches during its lifetime but there is a difference between signs of honest use and careless abuse. Neither a revolver nor an automatic will appreciate being laid down on a rough surface or left to slide around in the glove compartment of a car. In only a short time its high finish will be scratched and marred, destroying its quality appearance. It is true that small areas of the blueing of a well-kept gun will, in time, show signs of wear but there is no need to speed up the process unnecessarily.

Even the most strongly constructed automatic or revolver can be damaged if dropped or thrown on a hard surface. In the case of a revolver, if it lands on its cylinder there is a good chance that the crane may be sprung which will mean the attention of a good gunsmith to put it back into working order again. With some weapons, inadvertent dropping may cause *accidental firing* while parts such as sights and grips can be bent or split even if no other damage is incurred. A handgun does not make a good club in a fight in spite of what the Hollywood Westerns would have us believe. It is true that Western lawmen preferred the Colt Single Action revolver because it could be used subdue drunken cowhands and other trouble makers by 'Buffaloing' or 'Bending the Barrel' over their heads. This was a method favored by Wyatt Earp but the revolvers often suffered some damage as a result. His Colt Single Action needed two ejector rods and housings replaced because of this. Spinning a revolver around one's finger is another good way to ensure that it becomes damaged when you drop it. Such fancy tricks serve no useful purpose in gun handling and should be confined to circus performers. It can also be dangerous if you try it with a loaded handgun or one you forgot to unload. Quiet a novel way to shoot yourself!

Handguns should not be dismantled beyond the stage recommended by the manufacturer for normal cleaning and maintenance. Some people just have to take a firearm apart to see how it works. This is both stupid and senseless and many novices have done this only to find, on trying to reassemble it, that there are enough parts left over to make another firearm. Taking pistols apart is a job for an experienced gunsmith, not a novice.

The opening and closing of the cylinder of a solid frame sideswing revolver needs a special comment. The favourite trick of the film detective is to open and close the cylinder with a flick of the wrist. This looks very professional and impressive but in fact plays havoc with the revolver. The impact a heavy cylinder causes when treated thus can spring the frame so that the revolver goes out of time. A revolver's cylinder must be carefully opened by releasing the latch and easing out the cylinder with the forefinger. On closing, the cylinder must also be eased back into the frame under the control of the thumb and forefinger. NEVER ATTEMPT TO FORCE A CYLINDER OF A COCKED REVOLVER EITHER OPEN OR CLOSED. This can damage a revolver to such an extent that only a gunsmith can put it in working order.

Automatics are generally more robust and most problems seem to occur because of damaged magazines. These items are made of relatively thin steel plate and can easily be dented or damaged if dropped or treated roughly.

Cleaning

To function reliably, *handguns must be kept clean and free from dirt at all times.* This applies particularly to automatics which are more susceptible to stoppages due to dirt. Failure to clean guns after firing can also accelerate rusting and corrosion which can do irreparable harm.

Cleaning equipment and materials for handguns are relatively inexpensive and obtainable at all gunshops. The essential cleaning items are a rod of some suitable material, such as brass, that will not damage the bore; a bronze brush to suit the calibre of the gun; cleaning patches; good quality light oil; and possibly gun solvent to remove metal and powder fouling.

When a firearm is fired, particles of burnt powder and lead cause deposits to build up in certain areas which can, if not removed, cause malfunctions. Particles of lead or copper are sometimes left in the groves of the rifling by the bullet. In earlier times, the powder and primers used were corrosive and, if not cleaned out after firing, would very soon cause rusting. Modern ammunition does not have corrosive properties but this does not mean that cleaning is not necessary. The deposits of metal in the rifling must be removed before they build up to such an extent that the gun becomes inaccurate and, even though modern ammunition is not corrosive, rusting can still occur in dirty barrels.

Handguns need cleaning before and after firing. In either case, the first step is to *make quite sure that the gun is unloaded.* Don't become a front page headline of yet another gun owner accidentally killed while cleaning his gun. Once it has been made safe, your gun, if it is an automatic, should be field-stripped (taken apart) for cleaning. This usually means removing the slide from the frame and taking out the barrel. Side-swing revolvers have their cylinders swung open while break top designs are opened as for unloading.

Cleaning before firing involves wiping the barrel through with a clean patch using the rod to remove all traces of grease, oil and dirt. With a revolver, in addition to the bore, each cylinder chamber must also be cleaned in the same manner. All oil and grease must then be removed from the gun and it will be ready to shoot. Only the internal working parts and, in the case of an automatic, the slide rails, should be lightly oiled.

Cleaning after firing is a little more involved. After *unloading and making safe* begin by cleaning the bore. Wipe it through using a clean dry patch and examine it. Any signs of leading will mean that the bronze brush must be pushed through until all deposits have been removed. When a dry patch comes out clean after being pushed through the bore then, with a revolver deal with the chambers in the same manner. *Be careful not to use a patch too large* as it may become lodged in the barrel and require the services of a gunsmith to remove it.

Finally, all traces of fouling must be removed. In a revolver this is usually lodged around the barrel where it protrudes inside the frame and the front of the cylinder. In automatics it is usually found on the slide and frame rails, magazine well, breach face and under the extractor claw. A useful cleaning tool is an old toothbrush which can usually get into all the difficult places. Stubborn traces can be removed with the assistance of the solvent and tooth brush. Fouling on the cylinder face is often difficult to remove but light strokes with the bronze brush will usually do the trick.

Once clean, the bore and outside metal surfaces should be wiped over with an oily patch using a good light machine oil. If the gun is likely to be used, then it should have the oil removed afterwards. A light oil of the type used in sewing machines should be used throughout on slide rails on automatics and the internal parts of the revolver, as already mentioned. These parts should be only lightly oiled. Heavy oiling, unless the gun is to be stored for any length of time, will only pick up dirt and dust.

When the gun is to be stored it should be lightly oiled as described and left in this condition. It is important to make sure that not only the bore and chambers have a thin film of oil protecting them, but also all metal surfaces. In moist climates (coastal areas) guns must be frequently inspected to make sure they are not rusting. If a handgun has been exposed to water or moisture it must be completely dried and then well oiled — with regular inspections afterwards to ensure that it is rust free. Guns that are to be stored for extensive periods should be greased rather than oiled. Finally, *avoid storing handguns in leather holsters or plastic bags.* These often have considerable moisture in them and, in the case of plastic bags, water vapour often condenses on the plastic. The best storage is a clean box.

Maintenance

Through constant use certain parts of a handgun will wear and need to be replaced. You should have ample warning of this so that you can have your handgun serviced by a gunsmith at the appropriate time.

In automatics, magazines usually need to be replaced. Check them frequently for dents, cracks in the metal near the lips and bent or damaged lips. Safeties and barrel bushing also wear and need replacement.

In revolvers, the parts that usually need replacement are the hand which turns the cylinder and the bolt that locks the cylinder in place on firing. You should have some indication when this is likely to occur in the former if the cylinder does not completely line up when the trigger is pulled or the hammer cocked. Shooters next to you on the range who complain of being struck by minute shavings when you shoot could also be an indication! Don't mistake the fact that some Colt revolvers don't quite line up when the hammer is cocked. This is normal and the final alignment of the cylinder occurs when the trigger is pulled. If the cylinder skips (does not lock in place) or if the bolt starts to click into place soon after the cylinder begins to turn, this is a good indication that the bolt is worn and needs to be replaced. While there is always a little sideways movement in the cylinder when it is locked in place, if this becomes very loose a new bolt is probably needed.

A well-made automatic or revolver is a precision instrument of the highest quality and deserves to be kept clean and well maintained. Apart from this, you may have to stake your life on it one day so treat it like a good friend and look after it. It will, in return, repay you by not letting you down in your hour of need.

Appendix
Handgun Ammunition

This summary of handgun ammunition covers all of the popular calibers. It does not, however, include the many exotic types of ammunition used for specialized purposes like handgun hunting or long range Silhouette Shooting.

.22 Rimfire. This ammunition comes in three basic case lengths: Short, Long and Long Rifle. The Short is mainly used by Olympic Rapid Fire Shooters because of its mild recoil. The standard velocity Long Rifle round is also popular with target shooters, while the high velocity with hollowpoint bullets is considered a useful round for small game. The .22 Long does not see much use, being neither a target load nor one suitable for hunting.

Recent introduction of hyper velocity loads under brand names like 'Stinger' and 'Yellow Jacket' has increased the potency of the .22 even further. The most powerful rimfire round is the .22 Winchester Magnum Rimfire. With twice the case length of the .22 Long Rifle, it produces velocities close to 1,500 fps (feet per second) out of revolvers. Both the hyper velocity and the magnum are intended for hunting small game.

.25 ACP (Automatic Colt Pistol). Also called the 6.35 Browning, this is the smallest and least effective of the centerfire cartridges and is made for the tiny semi-automatic pistols.

.30 (7.63 mm) Mauser and .30 (7.65 mm) Luger. These two rounds are made for Mauser and Luger semi-automatic pistols. The former has the highest velocity of 1,410 fps which gives it great penetration ability. The Luger round does not have quite the same velocity and, although both are superior to the standard .32 ACP, they are still lacking in stopping power when compared to the larger calibers.

.32 ACP (Automatic Colt Pistol). This round is also known as the 7.65 Browning and is made for the numerous semi-automatic pocket pistols. While superior to the .25 ACP, it is still too small to be considered a reliable man-stopping round although its potency in this respect has been somewhat improved by the introduction of hollowpoint bullets like Winchester Silvertips.

.32 Short Colt; .32 Long Colt; .32 Colt New Police; .32 S&W and .32 S&W Long. These are all revolver cartridges that are about as effective as the standard .32 ACP. The .32 S&W Long is a very good target round and there are a number of European made semi-automatic target pistols made for it.

.380 ACP (Automatic Colt Pistol). This ammunition is also called 9 mm Short and is considered by many to be the minimum as far as defense loads go. There are a number of very good semi-automatic pistols made for this round and its effectiveness has been improved upon by the introduction of semi-jacketed hollowpoint bullets.

.38 Short Cased Revolver Ammunition. There is quite a range of short-cased .38 ammunition made for top break revolvers. Known by a variety of names like .38 Colt Short, .38 Colt New Police, and .38 S&W, they are under-powered and not as effective as the .380 ACP.

.38 Super. This is a very powerful cartridge for semi-automatic pistols that has never really caught on. Only a few pistols, like the Colt Government Model are chambered for it. When loaded with jacketed hollowpoint bullets, it is a good defense round.

9 mm Parabellum (9 mm Luger). Probably the most popular semi-automatic pistol cartridge, being used by the majority of the worlds militay forces. Although its velocity is in excess of 1,100 fps, its effectiveness as a defense round has been hampered by the use of jacketed round nose bullets. However, since it is now also available with a variety of expanding hollow-point bullets, its fight stopping ability has dramatically improved.

.38 Special (.38 S&W Special). The world's most versatile revolver cartridge and the first choice of target shooters and many police departments. Its ac-curacy is unquestioned although its ability to stop a determined attacker has often been questioned. However, its effectiveness has been greatly improved in recent years with the introduction of +P loads. These drive expanding semi-jacketed bullets at high velocities and, being more powerful than the standard loads, should not be used in many of the small framed revolvers.

.357 Magnum. Developed from the .38 Special, the .357 Magnum is an ex-cellent cartridge for defense and hunting. Revolvers chambered for it will also chamber .38 Special but the converse is not the case. Probably its greatest asset is the fact that a large selection of medium frame revolvers are chambered for this powerful round.

.41 Magnum. This cartridge was developed especially for law enforcement. It comes in two loads. One drives a 210 grain bullet at a velocity of 1,050 fps and is controllable with adequate stopping power. The other is more power-ful, having a velocity in the region of 1,500 fps. The .41 Magnum is an ex-cellent load for both self defense and hunting. Its only drawback is the fact that only large frame revolvers can handle it.

.44 Special (.44 S&W Special). This is a very accurate revolver cartridge that has a mild recoil yet good stopping power. Unfortunately, like the .41 Magnum, most revolvers chambered for it are large.

.44 Magnum. The king of handgun cartridges and an excellent hunting round. Its heavy recoil and the large size of the revolvers chambered for it makes it difficult for some to handle although revolvers chambered for it will also shoot the milder .44 Special.

.45 ACP (Automatic Colt Pistol). An excellent defense cartridge for those who favour the automatic having a reasonably mild recoil yet plenty of stop-ping power. It is also very accurate and is used by target shooters. Certain revolvers can also use it with clips. The Auto-Rim cased variety is made especially for revolvers.

.45 Colt. This historic old revolver cartridge is still popular today and is very good for defense. Like all of the other large calibers, only large revolvers are made for it.

BIBLIOGRAPHY
(And recommended further reading)

PISTOL SHOOTING IN GENERAL

SIXGUNS BY KEITH
Elmer Keith *(Stackpole)*

TEXT BOOK OF PISTOLS AND REVOLVERS
Colonel Julian S Hatcher *(Thomas Samworth)*

SIMPLIFIED PISTOL AND REVOLVER SHOOTING
Charles Edward Chapel *(Coward – McCann)*

DEFENSIVE PISTOL SHOOTING

FAST AND FANCY REVOLVER SHOOTING
Ed McGivern *(Wilcox & Follett)*

NO SECOND PLACE WINNER
Bill Jordan

COMBAT SHOOTING FOR POLICE
Paul B Wessen *(Charles C Thomas)*

COOPER ON HANDGUNS
Jeff Cooper *(Petersen)*

LAW ENFORCEMENT HANDGUN DIGEST
Dean Grennell & Mason Williams *(DBI Books)*

COMBAT HANDGUN SHOOTING
James D Mason *(Charles C Thomas)*

DER INTERNATIONALE POLIZEI-CONBAT-PARCOURS
Siegfried F Hübner *(Journal-Verslag,   Schwend GmbH,Schwäbish Hall)*

**NATIONAL RIFLE ASSOCIATION OF AMERICAN POLICE
INSTRUCTION MANUAL**
Various articles from;
The Federal Bureau of Investigation
Law Inforcement Bulletins

Law and Order Magazine

TARGET PISTOL SHOOTING

PISTOL SHOOTING AS A SPORT
Hans Standl *(Crown Pub.)*

PISTOL MARKSMANSHIP
United States Army Marksmanship Training Unit

PISTOL SHOOTING — AN INSTRUCTION MANUAL
National Small-bore Rifle Association of Great Britain

REVOLVER SHOOTING
Walter Winans *(G P Putman & Sons)*

FIREARMS HISTORY

EARLY PERCUSSION FIREARMS
Lewis Winant *(Jenkins)*

THE BOOK OF THE GUN
Harold L Peterson *(Hamlyn)*

FAMOUS GUNS FROM THE HAROLDS CLUB COLLECTION
Hank Wieand Bowman *(Fawcett)*

ANTIQUE GUNS FROM THE STAGECOACH COLLECTION
Hank Wieand Bowman *(Fawcett)*

BOOK OF PISTOLS & REVOLVERS
W H B Smith *(Stackpole)*

A HISTORY OF THE COLT REVOLVER
Charles T Haven and Frank A Belden *(Bonanza)*

SMITH & WESSON TIP-UP REVOLVERS
Profile Publications. Small-arms Profile 17

COLT CARTRIDGE REVOLVERS
Profile Publications. Small-arms Profile 20

WALTHER AUTOMATIC PISTOLS
Profile Publications, Small-arms Profile 6

SMITH & WESSON 1857-1945
Robert J Neal and Roy J Jenks *(A S Barnes)*

HANDGUN MAINTENANCE AND REPAIR

PROFESSIONAL GUNSMITHING
W J Howe *(Stackpole)*

COMPLETE GUIDE TO GUNSMITHING
Charles Edward Chapel *(Barnes)*

PISTOLSMITHING
Major George C Nonte *(Stackpole)*

HOME GUNSMITHING DIGEST
Tommy L Bish and Jack Lewis *(Gun Digest)*

ACCOUNTS OF PISTOL FIGHTS

THE GUNFIGHTERS
Dale T Schoenberger *(Caxton)*

THE AUTHENTIC LIFE OF BILLY THE KID
Sheriff Patrick Floyd Garrett *(Sphere)*

WYATT EARP — FRONTIER MARSHALL
Stuart N Lake *(Houghton Mifflin)*

DILLINGER DAYS
John Toland *(Mayflower)*

THE SEARCH FOR AN EFFECTIVE POLICE HANDGUN
Allan Bristow *(Charles C Thomas)*

CROWD AND RIOT CONTROL
Colonel Rex Applegate *(Stackpole)*

THE BOOTLEGGERS
Kenneth Allsop *(Arrow)*

THE GUNS OF THE GUNFIGHTERS
Guns and Ammo Book *(Peterson)*

OFFICER DOWN: CODE THREE
Pierce R Brooks *(Motorola)*

THE FOSTER GANG
Herzel Schlosberg and Ian Hamilton *(Heinemann)*

THE DEATH OF BILLY THE KID
John Poe *(True West Magazine)*

BUT ITS DEATH TO BONNIE AND CLYDE
Frontier Times Magazine

OLD TIMERS WORE 'EM HIGH
William Brent *(Guns Magazine)*

THE 1967 UNITED STATES PRESIDENTIAL COMMISSION ON LAW ENFORCE-MENT

Various articles from;
The Federal Bureau of Investigation Law Enforcement Bulletins Law and Order Magazine

Glossary of Terms

Accurize   Work done on a pistol to make it shoot more accurately.

A.C.P. (ACP)   Abbreviation for Automatic Colt Pistol e.g. 45 ACP refering to ammunition for Colt Government Automatic Pistol.

Air Pistol   A pistol that uses compressed air or gas to propel a pellet.

Anvil   Part of a primer assembly in a cartridge against which the priming compound is compressed when struck by the firing pin.

Backlash   The travel of the trigger after the hammer has been released. In good firearms there should be virtually no backlash.

Backstrap   The rear metal portion of a handgun grip.

Ball-ammunition   A reference to ammunition with a solid bullet.

Barrel Bushing   The bushing in the front of the slide of an automatic which holds the muzzle of the barrel.

Belly gun   A revolver with a short barrel (2 inches/50 mm)

Berden Primer   A cartridge ignition system invented by Colonel Berden where the anvil is part of the cartridge case.

Blank   A cartridge that does not have a bullet. Used in training or starting athletic events.

Blue   The Blue/Black oxide metallic finish given to firearms.

Bolt   Also called cylinder stop. A movable stud in the frame of a revolver that locks the cylinder in place when it is in line with the barrel.

Boxer Primer   A cartridge ignition system invented by Colonel Boxer that incorporates the anvil in the primer cap. This system is popular with reloaders.

Breech   The end of the bore into which the bullet enters.

Bulged barrel   A bulge in a barrel caused by excessive gas pressure when a shot is fired because of an obstruction in the bore.

Cant   Tilting a pistol sideways while aiming.

Checkering   Ornamental cross-cuts on certain portions of the metal and wood of a weapon cut with a file to help secure a better hold.

Clip   The magazine of an automatic pistol.

Compensator   A device fitted to the muzzle of a barrel that uses the escaping gases to reduce recoil by deflecting them upwards. Used in target pistols made for the Olympic Rapid Fire Discipline.

Conversion Unit   A set of major component parts that permit a pistol to fire ammunition of another calibre.

Crane   Also called 'yoke'. That part of the cylinder assembly of a solid frame revolver that swings the cylinder out of the frame for loading and unloading.

Cylinder latch   The catch in a revolver that permits the cylinder to be opened.

Cylinder stop   See bolt.

Disconnector   A device in an automatic pistol prevents firing unless the action is completely closed.

Disassemble   To dismantle a firearm for cleaning or repair.

Dud   A cartridge that fails to fire.

Ejection Port   The opening in the slide of an automatic pistol out of which the empty case is ejected.

Ejector   A device in an automatic pistol that expels the fired case as the slide moves rearwards.

Ejector Rod   The push-rod in a revolver used to eject fired cases from the cylinder.

Extractor   A claw-like device in an automatic pistol that withdraws a cartridge from the chamber when the slide moves to the rear.

Fanning   The quick firing of a single action revolver by slapping the hammer with the palm of the free hand while the trigger is held back.

Feed lips   The top portion of an automatic pistol's magazine that keep the rounds in place but allows them to move forward into the chamber during loading or firing.

Feed ramp   A ramp just under the barrel of an automatic that guides the nose of the bullets into the chamber during firing or loading.

Field strip   To dismantle a pistol for cleaning.

Flutes   Semi-circular cuts in the front of a revolver cylinder between the chambers to reduce weight.

Frame   The basic component of a firearm that houses the action or lockwork.

Gas Pistol   A pistol that uses gas, usually carbon dioxide, to propel a pellet.

Gauge   Used to measure accurately tolerances. In target shooting a gauge is used to check strikes on the target that are close to a scoring line.

Grip Safety   A device fitted to an automatic pistol and some revolvers that permits firing only when a positive grip is taken with the hand.

Half-cock   A position half way between rest and full cock in which the hammer of an automatic pistol or single action revolver can be held by the sear.

Half-moon clips   Clips in the shape of a half moon made of thin spring steel that permit automatic cartridges to be fired in certain revolvers.

Hammer Shroud   A shroud that fits onto or is an integral part of a revolver frame which prevents the hammer spur from snagging in clothing but still permits cocking the hammer for single action fire.

Hand   Also called 'pawl'. A lever that engages the ratchet of a revolver cylinder and turns it sufficiently to bring a chamber in line with the barrel.

Head Space   The distance between the breech face and that part of the chamber against which the cartridge bears.

Hollow point   Bullets which have a hole in the front to promote mushrooming on impact.

Jag   A round tip that fits onto the end of a cleaning rod to allow the fitting of a cleaning patch.

Jam   A malfunction in a firearm that prevents further firing until cleared.

Keyhole   The upsetting of a cartridge during firing, either in the barrel or while in flight, which causes it to strike the target sideways.

Knurling   The checkering on the metal parts of a firearm.

Lands and grooves   The rifling in the bore. Lands refer to the protrusions while grooves to the cuts.

Lanyard ring   A ring in the butt of a handgun that permits the attaching of a lanyard.

Leading   A build up of lead in the groves of rifling. Can usually be removed using a bronze brush on the end of a cleaning rod. Excessive leading can be detrimental to accuracy.

Loading gate   A catch, usually found in single action revolvers, that permits the cylinder to be loaded or unloaded.

Magazine Safety   A device fitted to some automatic pistols that prevents firing when the magazine is removed.

Magazine catch   A catch which permits the magazine to be released and is usually a button behind the trigger or a catch at the bottom of the grip.

Mainspring   The spring that drives the hammer forward to fire the weapon.

Mushroom   The upsetting of the bullet head on impact which causes it to expand beyond its normal diameter.

Muzzle	The front of the barrel out of which the bullet emerges on firing.
Muzzle Velocity	The velocity of a bullet the moment it leaves the muzzle.
Nipple	A protrusion fitted to percussion firearms over which the percussion cap is placed.
Partridge sights	A square front sight and rear sight with a rectangular notch which is popular in target shooting.
Peacemaker	A nickname for a Colt Single Action Army revolver.
Pellet	A missile fired by an air or gas pistol. Can also refer to the shot of a shotgun cartridge.
Ramp sight	A front sight that is mounted on a ramp. Usually, in handguns, the rear of the frontsight is angled or round to permit drawing from a holster.
Range	Can be either a place where firearms are fired in practice or the distance between the shooter and the target.
Range Discipline	Observance of the rules of a firing range.
Range Officer	Person in command of shooters on a firing range.
Ratchet	The notches in the rear of a revolver cylinder which, when engaged by the hand, turn it to bring a chamber into line with the barrel.
Recoil	The rearward motion of a firearm caused by the discharge of a round.
Recoil Shield	A circular plate in a revolver frame that prevents the cartridge from falling out.
Reloads	Cartridges that have been recharged.
Safety Catch	A manually operated catch which, when applied, prevents the weapon from being fired. Rarely found on revolvers.
Sear	A lock or catch that holds the hammer or firing pin in place when cocked.
Service Match	A competition where only service weapons are used.
Service Pistol	A handgun designed for military or police use.
Side arm	A handgun.
Sizing	A method used in the reloading of ammunition to give either a cartridge case or a bullet its correct diameter.
Slide Stop	A lever in an automatic pistol that holds the slide open, usually after the last round has been fired. Allows the slide to go forward when depressed.
Small Bore	A term used to denote a small calibre, usually .22
Smokestack	A malfunction in an automatic pistol where the case has not been fully ejected and is lodged between the barrel and the slide.
Spitting	The shaving off of portions of a bullet in a revolver during firing which indicates that the cylinder is not lining up correctly.
Sub-calibre	A term used in Practical Pistol Shooting to denote calibre under 38 special or 9 mm.
Trigger Shoe	A shoe that fits onto the front of the trigger to make it wider.
Trigger stop	A stop that prevents the trigger from travelling further back than is necessary after the hammer has been released.
Wadcutter	A bullet with a flat head that is popular in Centre Fire Target shooting.
Windage	The lateral adjustment of sights.
X-Ring	An additional ring inside the centre scoring circle of a target that is used to break ties between competitors, i.e. where a number of competitors have the same score the one with the greatest number of shots inside the X-ring will be the winner.
Yoke	See crane.
Zero	To adjust sights so that the shots will strike at the point of aim.

INDEX